No. 9 ‡ Summer 2018

Edited by S. T. Joshi

The spectral realms that thou canst see
With eyes veil'd from the world and me.

H. P. LOVECRAFT, "To a Dreamer"

SPECTRAL REALMS is published twice a year by Hippocampus Press,
P.O. Box 641, New York, NY 10156 (www.hippocampuspress.com).
Cover illustration and design by Daniel V. Sauer, dansauerdesign.com.
Hippocampus Press logo by Anastasia Damianakos.

ISBN 978-1-61498-228-9   ISSN 2333-4215

Contents

To Michael Fantina
1948–2018
in memoriam

Poems

The Visionary

Ian Futter

His home is drab and dingy, but
his dreams are sharp and clear.
Two demons are his fondest friends;
anxiety and fear.

His frantic thoughts are shackled to
the fetters of his bliss.
He raves at what he thinks he sees,
and what he sees is this:

A hull that's split and splintered
on a ship beneath the sea,
where all the dream-dead sailors writhe
and rot eternally.

A captain, pale and clammy,
sea lice gnawing at his skin,
with corpse-eyes fixed upon the deep
and all that squirms within.

He sees the captain's hair, which mocks
Medusa with each tide.
He sees the hands upon the wheel
at which the captain died.

He sees the captain's head jerk back;
a puppet to a wave.
The sailors twisting in their tomb—
an animated grave.

He sees their mouths; all open caves
for fish to swim within.
He sees a fish swim past a book
beneath the captain's chin.

The book is all bedraggled in
black tunic, dank and torn;
but as he stares he sees the shapes
on parchment, wet and worn.

He strains to read the scribbles and
the script of ancient text.
He mumbles as he mouths the words
on which his mind is vexed.

He does not know the language, so
the meaning is obscure.
The sounds, which consonants consume,
are troubling to endure.

And so he dips his pen to ink
and copies, as he reads,
this manuscript from fathoms deep,
in wreck amongst the weeds.

And as he writes, he sees the captain
and the crew once more;
alive upon their fated ship,
so lately from the shore.

He sees the captain take the book
into his cabin, dark.
He hears the ancient words intoned,
while stolid sailors lark.

He sees the dimming sky reveal
the paleness of the craft;
He hears the waters smash against
the ship, both fore and aft.

And soon the captain, cloaked in black,
emerges on the deck.
He grins to see his fearful crew
and preaches of the wreck

and ruin that will consume this ship
and drag them far below.
He preaches of immortal death,
which only he can know.

He preaches of their sacrifice
and beasts that came before;
He tells them of his arcane book,
which opens ancient doors.

The sailors plead and pray unto
a God who doesn't hear.
The captain reads aloud the words
that petrify their ears.

And soon they hear a rumble and
a roar beneath the keel,
and as stained shadows seize the ship
the captain takes the wheel.

He hears the captain laughing, as
the screams engulf the deck.
He sees the crew all dead once more
and bloated in the wreck.

And as this vision fades his eyes
alight upon his scrawl,
where shadows leap from darkening page
to rest upon the wall.

Framed by his window stands a man
whom he has seen before;
consumed by creatures 'neath the waves,
now knocking at his door.

He hears the bubbling breathing of
the thing that lurks outside;
His door an opening coffin lid
from which he cannot hide.

And as the door with creaks and cracks
Is opened from the gloom,
the soaked and sodden shape limps in—
rogue relic from its doom.

This mockery of movement, all
foul flesh replete with leaks,
advancing still on stagnant steps
through groans and gurgles speaks.

"My ship is lost and sunken. All
the crew are drowned below,
and I will drag you to the depths,
where all the dead must go."

Damp fingers prod his dripping bones
till finding what he needs,
he slips the slimy volume out;
spits water as he reads.

The dreamer writhes and wriggles
as he watches through his tears.
He cannot block the captain's voice
or smother what he hears.

He hears the water rushing and
the sailors' gargling screams.
He feels the shadows flood his mind
and blacken out his dreams.

And when the morning's broken and
the dark has morphed to light,
They find him, rigid in his chair;
Dead dreamer, drowned with fright.

Final Library

Ann K. Schwader

A palimpsest repurposed from some past
lost manuscript—*well lost*—its surface shone
illuminated. Sacred writings vast
& vacant with ape-faith had overgrown
that void once offered to a Voice unknown
by any mortal name. Yet what it spoke
still echoed there to summon shadows flown
from darker stars than ours, & worlds that broke
beneath their wings.   Indelible, they soaked
through layered ignorance to snare the gaze
of some wise idiot—who then uncloaked
each syllable, each fatal turn of phrase,
& called it scholarship. The sky outside
cracked black with nightmares as our last hope died.

Flesh Flowers

John Shirley

Deep beneath the canopies
of ancient, shadowy
rainforest trees,
in a certain valley
where hot springs steam:
No human strays there
unless they have need—
for the flesh flowers growing
like Dali's dreams.

Flesh flowers . . . are not fresh flowers;
they open wide to all who dare;
Flesh flowers are open all hours—
their musky fragrance chokes the air.

In the concrete jungle
they transplant and grow
in every skin color
—in a living glow;
They writhe and they beckon,
they drip with nectar:
any drop that's given
is hungrily taken.

Are you using them?
O, they're using you—

they're twining your leg,
then growing from you;
are they symbiotes
or parasites?
They're both at once—
they consume living light.

Flesh flowers—scarcely fresh flowers;
they open wide to all who dare.
Flesh flowers—they're open all hours;
their musky fragrance chokes the air . . .

Forty Years in Innsmouth

M. F. Webb

To live as lighthouse wife—some called it doom;
A future once enormous bound, then shrinking,
But I loved him enough to brave the chill
To trade the busy square for sky and ocean.
'Twere secret then to me the shoreline rites
And Obed Marsh's love of things abhorred.

Away from town and farm, those priests abhorred
Were distant shapes that threatened secret doom,
And if my friends and kin engaged those rites,
I did not know, my past relations shrinking.
To me, their absence was a greater chill
Than any spawned near monstrous sky or ocean.

Then loneliness gave way to greater chill
As his obsession swelled with the abhorred,
Dull hours spent with a spyglass trained on ocean,
Determined to preserve the lost from doom.
He could not see his greater purpose shrinking
As in his way he fell prey to their rites.

I cannot say if these were devil rites,
Although their crazed abandon struck a chill
Which shuddered through my soul and left me shrinking.
Perhaps 'twas just their strangeness I abhorred,

The unfamiliar chants portending downfall
The priests and supplicants beside the ocean.

Till years of tending beacons by the ocean,
Protecting foundered ships from demon rites,
Convinced me that we two faced certain doom
If only from past neighbors now turned chill,
As we ourselves became the ones abhorred,
The safety of our lighthouse dimmed and shrinking.

And seeing all my hope and promise shrinking
I resolved to flee far from the ocean
Far from all my husband now abhorred.
I begged of him to disregard the rites,
To seek a warmer clime, forswear the chill—
Yet still he ruminates on others' doom.

I—rather than embrace impending doom
From land or ocean dark entombed and chill,
Our past abhorred—have left him to his rites.

A Dream of Vengeance

(In Imitation of Robert E. Howard)

Michael Fantina

Huge cities burn on the midnight plain;
Pale riders gallop to north and south.
I wander dreams in a driving rain
And dream of a harlot's pink-lipped mouth.
Great schooners burn in the harbor there
While their flames, mast-high, are yellow, red,
And acrid is this smoked filled air.
The king lies in his palace—dead.

Tribes of the east are raging ever;
Their savage numbers sweep all before.
Hideous they, and passing clever,
They burn and pillage fen and moor.
There in the dark a ghost is eyeing
These beasts of men who have their way.
In ruthlessness is each man vying,
Drunk with the urge to burn and slay!

Only this ghost may stay or stall them;
She once a wizard dark and drear,
Only she who may lure and call them.
In her silk gown she will appear!
Strides in the darkness tall and regal,
Gathers the tribes before her then.

They stand aghast, know she is lethal;
They flee from her to the nearby fen.

There in the shadows slays them slowly;
She cuts them down both left and right.
Vengeance is hers and is hers only,
Her arrows slay them there in flight!
Only their chieftains now are ringing
Her around in the loamy soil.
Her eyes flash redly, now they're cringing,
They are dispatched, to end her toil.

Huge cities burn on the midnight plain;
Pale riders gallop to north and south.
I wander dreams in a driving rain
And dream of a harlot's pink-lipped mouth.
Great schooners burn in the harbor there
While their flames, mast-high, are yellow, red,
And acrid is this smoked filled air.
The king lies in his palace—dead.

The Thing in the Forest
A Revbaiyat

Frank Coffman

Now is the wind grown wild. Gnarled branches sway;
Barren in winter's death, they wave and creak.
It seems the End Year's chance quite to repay
Summer's gold heat and warmly green spring day.

And traveling through this woodland, blighted, bleak,
A man plods on, braving the numbing blast.
Many have sought before his goal to seek:
To find and kill a horror, a monstrous freak.

It is a legend from dark depths of Past,
A beast that holds dominion in that Wood—
A region of dark secrets, wide and vast.
To hunt the Thing, he's sworn he'll be the last.

The Thing, 'tis said, is last of all its brood—
In a line of horrors, it is the final horror.
He pulls his cloak more closely—and his hood.
He thinks out loud: "The beast's of flesh and blood.

"So it can die—despite the evil lore
That says it's magical and can't be slain."
On through that weird Wood, white with snow and hoar,
Until he comes upon a scene of gore.

The snow around that heap still keeps the stain
Of scarlet dulled—'round what had been a man—
From torn clothing, flecked by a bloody rain,
He knows his brother's quest has been in vain.

Fresh tracks still showed how his death fray began:
The creature's tracks, enormous, showed quite clear.
He'd briefly stood his ground, but turned and ran,
And now his shredded corpse lay cold and wan.

Just then, he knows the Thing is coming near.
He draws his sword and fits arm to his shield.
Soon, through the thick undergrowth, he can hear
Its passage. And he strives to stanch his fear.

"I will not fail. I'll stand my ground, not yield."
He girds his thoughts and readies for the fight.
And now the hideous creature is revealed!
And now he knows that his fate too is sealed!

Full twice his height and blacker than the night,
With gaping maw and massive antlered head,
With claws like knives, long slavering fangs of white,
It strides toward him in the waning light.

Now in the villages 'round that place 'tis said:
"*Let no one challenge the Damned Thing of the Wood!*
The bravest of our brave ones now is dead!"
The proof, thrown from the Wood . . .

     . . . his bloody, scream-locked head.

The "Revbaiyat" is a form invented by the present poet. Essentially it is
poem written in "reverse rubai." The original *rubai* stanza rhymes AABA.
The Persian original—as in Edward FitzGerald's famous *Rubaiyat of Omar
Khayyam*—and all rubaiyats are sequences of rubai. The "revbai" or
"reverse rubaiyat stanza" rhymes ABAA. This poem is an interlocking
revbaiyat rhyming ABAA BCBB CDCC, etc.

The Urge to Write

Liam Garriock

Sweltering, lost in deep thought, the poet sits at his desk with pen and paper, his mind feverishly teeming with satyrs and mortal gods and dark forests and angels. Dark creatures, like infernal nanites, stream through his veins and control his arms and numb his legs. His red hands violently tremble, and his burning temple throbs hideously; his yellowed teeth tightly clench, and the veins on his neck and face bulge like invasive serpents. The pen stands on the blank white paper, trembling eagerly, then trembling uneasily. The manic phantasies that his poor, crammed mind harbours struggle to be controlled, and they howl and clamour for release. They have made him shun the light of day, made him detest the burning summer sun outside. They have turned him against other people, whose ephemeral company he secretly yearns for. No matter how hard he tries to suppress them, they always return like cockroaches. But poor poet! What can he do whilst the manifold demons in his skull scream and shout and dance chaotically?

His teeth threaten to shatter like glass, and his bloodshot eyes threaten to burst out of their sockets. As his heart beats furiously, like a drum rapped by an impossibly fast spirit, the poet shoots up and lets out one final strained groan before collapsing to the floor. As his head hits the ground, it cracks and shatters like an egg, and out of his fractured skull, riding on a rancid river of ink, spill forth the manic beings born from his haunted imagination: all the clowns and homunculi and malign and maggoty ghosts and demons and leering fauns spread, like a swarm of locusts, to the outer world, withering the grass and flowers, darkening the sun and the verdant forests, freezing the lakes and rivers and seas, and rotting the souls of the living and resurrecting the decaying dead, until all the world is held in the unwavering grip of an eternal autumn.

The Sorceress's Lament

Ashley Dioses

The towering walls I built were only meant
To save myself from love's most tiresome songs.
My melodies so soon became laments
When my soft heartstrings for his tune did long.

Too deeply falling is a fault I bear,
For love, to me, is bound not by life's trifles.
Yet even so, as strong a love he shares,
Within him now, his feelings he would stifle.

The talk of magic, love and journeys, fights—
I thought that he was like the knights of old!
The high walls all but fell for such a sight—
But I then learned they were just stories told.

The fairy tales wrought from my few ideals
Left me so sad they were not realistic.
Knights gave no chase if it did not appeal
To schedules tightly made and so simplistic.

And yet I always had believed in them;
I traveled past far lands and sought out quests.
I have healed wounds with magick where they stem;
The love I saved from sadness was a test.

And now I fight the weakness gnawing me.
Such heavy blows my heart has surely taken,
And though my love for him not once did flee—
My heart was rattled and my soul was shaken.

He was no knight in armor, but a bard;
For stories he revealed he had the mind.
I was the knight at arms who would get charred—
I have the true heart that he needs to find.

Cornflower Valley

Christina Sng

The valley of the green
And blue washed away
Into the sea last night.

Along with it,
My home and my family—
Everything I have ever known.

Atop the mountain
I watch the world
Slowly dissipate

As my hands
Press down firmly
Onto the ground.

It shakes like a fearful child,
Rumbling as I summon
Earth golems to awake

And bring me
The alchemists
Who took my home.

In a circle they stand,
Heads bowed, hands tied
Behind their robes,

Silent while
I demand a reason
For their actions.

I reach to the sky
And grasp lightning bolts,
Sending each one

Through their bones
Till they are ashes
I press into the ground.

Soon the grass returns
And cornflowers sprout
All through the valley.

With each bud,
I bring back my family.
With each bud,

I bring back my home.

The Willful Child

Fred Chappell

"To spoil the children, spare the rod":
Falsely attributed to God,
This proverb, honored in days of yore
                  As sacred lore.

The child who was obedient
Smoothly to Paradise was sent,
If mournful circumstance applied
                  And the wee one died.

In cases where the child was willful,
Sullen, stubborn, smartass, baleful,
A different story would unfold
                  And often told:

One small girl, whose tyrant mother
Could not control her, was a bother
Of the most vexatious kind
                  To soul and mind.

When she was twelve a raging fever
Took away this girl forever;
But, lying dead, she raised her arm.
                  Cause for alarm!

To the graveyard then they hurried;
There the child was quickly buried;
They shoveled dirt and tamped it flat
                    And that was that.

Or so they thought. From her repose
Within the ground her arm arose,
Her wrist and hand and, *cause for anger,*
                    Her middle finger.

The mother grasped her birchen rod;
Down the road she swiftly trod;
At the grave she sharply caned
                    That impudent hand.

The hand withdrew from mortal sight,
But infected the rod with a birchen blight.
The mother shuddered and recoiled,
Fearing *the rod the child had spoiled*
                    With her dark might.

                    —*Grimm's Fairy Tales,* 534

Cat Girl Cantata

Michael D. Miller

This night hour
Entwined in bark and leaf
Touch of breath upon naked skin
Patches of damp weeds under feet
Glare of eyes tear against the moon
This prowling silence
This stillness
This quaking tremble of blood and veins
We create a thousand twisting trees
Snapping in the quake of our gravity
Till the dew of dawn
Over everything
Ever in the whispered rapture of your song

A Voyage Too Far

J. T. Edwards

Navigating the seas of a dead sun
Passing through sublime uncharted nebulae
Caught in the vacuum of a black sepulchre
Spiraling through million colored, hallucinatory, vortexes of time
Torn apart by cyclopean rat-faced gods
Every thought ever conceived
Locked in a casket of dreams

Are We Not Beautiful in Our Decay?

Allan Rozinski

The plague has raged the world over:
an unquenchable fire.
The infected surrender
to the unyielding demand
that its subjects partake
in the unholy feast,
making men into monsters
that hunger for human flesh
and nothing more.

I stand by her grave. For me,
rites of spring have long passed,
with constant signs of downward descent,
gravity pulling me ever lower,
to finally lie with my cold beloved
and meld with the soil that welcomes us
with a silent, cannibal call.

The dark earth seeks a final embrace . . .
an incestuous merger,
an orgy,
with dirt and vermin, microbes, spores,
forcing our rotten bodies
to release

their hold on life,
to yield what juices remain
before dissolving
into the nameless crust;
to join the layers upon layers
of timeless strata,
where no memories live,
where neither tears nor laughter
were ever known,
where no eyes have ever
witnessed and wondered upon
the joys and mysteries of life,
nor wept and cursed its
cruelest verdicts,
issued by a demonic
harlequin god
that revels in bringing
chaos from the void.

The Song of the Siren

Chelsea Arrington

Come home, come home, you sailors fair!
Come home to sleep in arms of dew.
I'll show you warmth beyond compare;
I'll be your mistress, rare and true.

Come lie in my arms and know love sweet;
Come sleep and dream here at my breast.
I'll wash and bathe your weary feet.
By Aphrodite, my hands are bless'd.

Ithaca calls and beckons your names,
Your hearth fires blazing bright and warm.
Forget the trickster's ill-timed games;
You will not fare another storm.

(Blackened corpses adorn my shore:
Putrescence upon which I tread
Is naught but just a little gore.
Do not distress your dear swab's head.)

Your mothers' voices are in my song;
Your sisters' and your brothers' too.
Give in to me, it won't take long;
Just swim through the deep and the darkest blue.

Acrostic Sonnet in Memory of Providence, R.I., 8 August 1936

Charles Lovecraft

Eternity your gaze is fixed upon,
Deep as the eons and the waves of night.
Grand are your dreams, whose shades of meaning on
A quilted landscape world with time unite.
Reaching for the unearthly 'world's a stage,'
Advancing knowledge with your well-wrought page,
Largely your beaconed profile flares your might.

Later men came to tear apart your deeds.
All failed. You are remaining on, their dust
Never above your ankles, or the weeds.
Provided by the spheres, your scent of must
Outpours in lonely rooms, a spectral vow:
Every secret is your cosmic bough.

A Bloodless Man

Mary Krawczak Wilson

Your vestments were black—like a priest;
You worshipped at the altar of death.
You offered blood instead of wine
And bones instead of bread.

At night you roamed the cloisters and catacombs,
And graced graveyards filled with tombs and bones.
Your nocturnal wanderings
Nourished your famished soul.

You were always searching for a sign or a symbol
That would take you back to a time never known—
A time when the world was ineffable and unknown—
A time before humans had yet to be born.

You abhorred the holy exorcists
Because they tried to tread into your realm—
The realm of evil—
An evil that flowed through your bloodless veins
Like a cancerous cyst
And continues to grow for all eternity.

Great Mother

David B. Harrington

Disregard the Great Mother and she'll disregard you when it comes time to suckle her breasts. You who hover above her while your bones turn to dust in her belly, have you forgotten her as well? Do her loving arms fasten you down as you wander aimlessly in the Land of Shadow longing to be free, where nobody has substance and nothing to sustain them but gravity itself?

Remember, then, the softness of your Mother's warm caress when she nestled you close to her bosom and brushed gently against your cheek. Remember how you once slumbered peacefully in her womb and dreamt of a hopeful renewal? Remember, as you lie paralyzed in the stench of her bowels, the richness of her beauty and the fragrance of her flowery folds: the sweet aroma of roses and cherry blossoms, laced with lilac.

So come, all you blood drinkers and flesh-eaters, to the Banquet of the Great Mother! Watch how she trembles and shakes as you cut her to pieces and gnaw at her flesh. Then burn her with fire and laugh in her face, leaving her to smolder in ash.

Feel her icy breath upon you like a cold winter frost, O you who strip away her dignity and rip apart her veil: for even now her sorrows are mounting.

Go ahead: bind her wrists, chain her ankles. Poke her with needles and stick her with pins! But beware, children, it is because of you that our Mother is enraged.

She is as wroth as a cosmic dragon: Feel her fiery breath upon you like a hot desert storm. Her lungs are clogged with thick black smoke that fumes from her nostrils, rising up to overwhelm her. The four winds swirl around her, one for every season. Can you hear them whisper her name?

So go ahead, plant your orchards and vineyards while her skin is still moist, O you who blind her eyes and leave her naked and shivering in the sun to die: for even now her teardrops are falling.

Behold your Mother's glory and kiss her on the cheek. Lift the burden that weighs so heavy on her shoulders. She was once a lovely young celestial virgin, pure and unspoiled, in a garden paradise bursting with ripened fruit, sweet and delicious.

But how we ravish her like wild animals, who can blame her for rebelling? How much more can she withstand, this Mother of ours, whom we cast aside like a used-up whore, all trampled and torn?

Has she not sung us tender lullabies and rocked us gently to sleep in cradles of swan feathers and pine needles? Be kind to your Mother and treat her with respect, I tell you! Why must you thrust her full of holes? Just how much venom must you sink into her veins before she becomes immune and rises up to swallow us like a viper?

Step out into the light, O you children of darkness, and cover your eyes with coal. Step out of the darkness, all you children of light, with your lamps trimmed way down low.

See how your Mother feeds the beasts of the field and the creatures of the forest that assemble at her feet, some by day some by night.

The lion, jackal, and wildebeest come from miles around just to drink out of her hands and taste her crystal-clear waters. The birds of the air nestle in her hair and the fish course through her veins to and fro the heart of her ocean.

Call to mind how she once flowed with milk and honey, and with wine. And now, even in her old age, she is pleased to nourish us with all the essentials of life.

What is it that is wrong with us? Are we no better than the hounds and vultures who will be left to lick at her wounds and lap up her blood, or will we rescue her in time to save ourselves? I think not.

Three Witches

David Barker

Three witches in a pasture stood—
one in a cape, one in a hood,
and one clad only
in the skin of a lonely
wolf who was slain
where the deacon's wife had lain
with the son of a farmer
who didn't mean to harm her.
Her sin declaimed aloud,
she was roundly disavowed.

The witch in a cape
grabbed a cat by the nape
deep in a wood
where the three witches stood,
and gave it to the witch
who was thought to be good.
That witch thrashed the cat
with a wooden baseball bat,
then wandered wide in search
of a place to discard
puss's body bruised and scarred—
she chose a shuttered church.

*   *   *

In a glade three witches stood—
one was bad, one was good,
and one was either,
or perhaps she was neither.
They danced in a pasture
underneath the harvest moon,
singing praises to Hastur,
echoed by a distant loon.

There the witch in wolf's skin
pledged to revel and to sin,
embraced her deep affinity
for voluptuous iniquity,
swore to practice excess,
although it always left a mess.

This youngest of the crones
to be born of the goat,
with her silver-bladed knife
cut the farm boy's throat
and dumped his flesh and bones
in the town's deep murky moat

to avenge the deacon's wife
at the cost of his life.

Then traipsing across the hills,
all three sisters got their thrills
by cavorting with Pan's Son,
ties and buttons all undone,
and they sang a song to Hastur
as they twirled in the pasture.

Angry in His Grave

Darrell Schweitzer

So we buried him,
angry in his grave,
our friend, rival, mentor, master,
for all he'd opened up to us
the glory and terror
of worlds beyond,
for all he made us what we are,
when you'd think we should have been grateful,
we stuffed him into his grave,
because the literally goddamned fool
had bartered away,
not his soul, not his blood,
not even our souls and blood,
but the most precious gift of all,
his own death,
and so he would have gone on forever,
with his thunderings and his conjurations,
and dragged us on forever,
had we had not buried him like that,
and he lies there, cursing,
angry in his grave,
and we know that he can never rest.

Toads

Wade German

Have gathered at the breeding pond,
Enormous, bloated and obscene:
A million mottled sickly green,
All from this very bog were spawned.

Ill moonlight glances off each back.
One rises out of murk, and wet
With slime suggesting fever-sweat,
It blinks, then sinks beneath the black.

Along the banks their choir croaks
Abysmal litanies, while clouds
Of noxious vapours sting the eyes;

While one great specimen, quite proud
And puffed-up, solemnly invokes
Foul prayers to gods which govern flies.

The Witch's Son

Adam Bolivar

There was a witch called Betty Crow
    Who had a son named Jack;
The thing about them both you know:
    Their hearts were cruel and black.

Their hearts was black, as were their souls,
    For they were devil's kin;
And for these two no church bell tolls,
    Their lives immersed in sin.

At night the graveyard they would haunt,
    A mother and her son,
Where they their wickedness could flaunt,
    Their wrongs espied by none.

But owls who perched in bare-branched trees
    And by the silver moon,
While whistled by a chilling breeze,
    For winter's time was soon.

And of their rites I dare not speak:
    They summoned things below,
By speaking Latin, and in Greek,
    Which both of them did know.

In course of years old Betty died,
    But Jack is still alive,
And if in you I may confide:
    Her corpse he yet may swive.

Halloween Reverie

K. A. Opperman

With every Halloween
That sadly goes a-passing,
The autumn leaves amassing
On lawns that once were green,
I know I'm growing older—
The poignant purple smolder
Of sunset burns more keen
On Halloween.

With every Halloween
That vanishes in shadows
While glow the twilight meadows
With jack-o'-lantern sheen,
The summer fades behind me—
I hope that you will find me
In some far, dim demesne
On Halloween.

Contemplate the Alchemy of Dancing Quantum Particles

Kendall Evans

Contemplate the Alchemy of Stars, planets
    Moons and asteroids
During an ordinary mundane
                     work day
Meditate upon the dance
               of quantum particles
Within the dizzy spin of
      the vast and ever-slowly spiraling
Spiral galaxies—
Imagine the hungry black hole
        there at the center of our own galaxy
& consider yourself blessed

Rek-Cocci Stirs

Scott J. Couturier

Rek-Cocci stirs—
Old, nefarious worm.
Deep in subterrene slumber,
its segments flex, secrete,
a repellent corpse-white epiderm.

Rek-Cocci, grand devourer.
It That Swallowed The Second Moon.
Writhing, the cadaveric mass bucks
against a stalactite-studded roof,
pain dispelling the dregs of its millennial swoon.

Rek-Cocci, ever-starving,
Dark-Haunter, Gorger of Graves.
Threading the earth like a loathly root,
it shivers, bleeds, roused from senescence;
vermiculate ichor the coarse stone veritably laves.

Rek-Cocci, coffin-worm incarnate,
revered of Eld in abominate temple-deeps.
Now, a centuried ritual is performed above:
living blood offered up by unliving hand.
Through porous stone the unhallowed effluence seeps.

Rek-Cocci, blind unsufferable god,
idiot avatar of the atavismal Void.

Lubricated by its leaking wounds
& energized by lich-rite goety,
it bores upwards, seeking the black magician thus employed.

Rek-Cocci, the Mindless Dreamer,
long disregarded as primitive, uncouth lore.
The dead god breaches the temple-close,
sundering flagstones, displacing altar & sacrifice:
its blood-garbed summoner falls prostrate, pressing fleshless face to floor.

Rek-Cocci, long-abandoned blight,
grown dim in annals penned on hides of human flesh.
Compelled by unreverent sorcery
to abide by the bidding of that once-mortal,
it knows hot wrath, and a maggot's yearning to return to its chasmal crèche.

Rek-Cocci, sense-organ of entropy,
sovereign of dead cycles & decay's rank succulence.
Yawning a tine-lined maw, it spews acidic fetor before
devouring the nameless necromancer, swiftly digesting desiccate viscera
before burrowing back to the nameless Dark, its passage holing
apocalyptic rents.

The Loved

Ian Futter

I keep you in a cabinet
at the bottom of the stairs.
Its glass has never tarnished
with the passing of the years.

Its locks, both sealed and fastened,
only open with one key;
my key,
affixed to my chain
for a stalled eternity.

Each hour I sit and gaze
upon the husk held in this case,
where cracks within your crumbling skull
hold memories of a face.

A face shrunken and shrivelled,
all corruption to my gaze,
yet sunken in decaying depths,
your eyes, fixated, blaze.

Fixated on my fingers, on my key
and on my face.
Fixated on the chain, you pull,
which binds me to this place.

Antarktos Sequence

Manuel Pérez-Campos

The polychrome ice crazily engulfing them
is supple and exact in its ensorcelments.
Stopping is unsustainable in any
direction. Aeons are grafted to each
step as the six in parkas and slit goggles
forego thought of apothegm and anthem
and learn to outgrow sublunary rites
of pretend aplomb. This is an annex
of hell which multiplies cliffs and cataracts
to keep itself a solitude: and as
they ramble into an ever-shifting
inconclusion, dreaming their deaths beneath
the gloom of a midnight sun, they become
coheralds of its eerie magnitude.

On a Poet's 80th Birthday

(*for Fred Phillips, 17 September 2017*)

Leigh Blackmore

Best blessings on thy day of days,
On length of life fit to amaze!
Eighty full years from birth till now—
My brother bard, to thee I bow!

In far Manhattan you repose
As from your pen weird dreaming flows,
As from the cauldron steams thy Muse
And to thy psyche gives dark clues.

O! Antient Sire of the Drowned Rat
Hunting the book thy habitat;
O! Student of the abstruse tome—
What light reflecteth from thy dome!

Companion of the noble cat—
Maya and Inca, sleek and fat;
O! Master of thine own domain,
With books and songs thy spirit's lain.

The winds from Sheol thou command,
Their darkling forces 'neath thy hand
With wizard way verse does outpour;
A toast to hundreds, thousands more!

Spectral Realms: An Homage

Frank Coffman

In this bright journal dark poets find a home,
A place for all reflections of *the Weird*.
Bedecking pages of this twice-yearly tome
Are spectres of both old- and new-to-be-feared
Offspring of many bold imaginations
That come to sharp focus as their weird is neared.
Yes, through these turn-churning paginations
Are woven the thoughts and stylings of bold minds:
Poets who dare to speculate. The ruminations
Of those who know that seeking often finds
The visions seen before by very few.
Yes, through these pageways, a weird river winds
Down from rich sources, merging to come in view:
A rushing torrent of the spectral new.

The Angel's Pen

Charles D. O'Connor III

When I opened my bloodshot eyes, an angel hovered above me. She wore silk garments studded with many-colored jewels, and golden hair—like fleece—ran down her back, touching wings mightier than the griffin's. But the most astounding feature lay in her face, where I saw the trace of an existence I thought I knew, and that I might one day know again. It was bright and lovely, like a million gardens of enchantment. I had to return and become part of its blissful magic. So, surrendering unto the angel, I fixed my gaze on her glorious countenance.

In her hand she held a pen:

"My special child, will you not take this and write soliloquies for the world?"

I smiled and took the pen, ready to bless the hearts of men.

But when I held the instrument in my hand, the angel howled and shook herself, mad with glee. She tore apart her face, glaring, gloating at me; that which was exposed was all brown pus, slimy bone—wet shards of flesh hanging at the ends.

"Take the pen and stab yourself in the heart. Blood will gush from its wounds like a river, and your brain will rot with madness. Each succeeding day you shall suffer pain—the pain needed to live. With this you will hurt other people, break women's hearts, and make your parents weep, wishing you were never born. There will be no recompense. You will lead a lonely life, for this is what you deserve. And you will die if you don't use the pen, experiencing its pain every waking moment. Your tormented life will entertain, but then be worth nothing in the end. My master's chosen ones—the happy, the successful, those who enjoy life's luscious fruits—they must be satiated by your suffering. So I command you: stab yourself with the pen, write words that will fall on deaf ears, make a spectacle of yourself, then wither away into obscurity and die. This is the only way for you to live."

After the angel finished, she disappeared, leaving the pen in my hand. But her words continued—booming, echoing, never letting me rest. I became a sad, lonely child, inflicted with a sickness of the soul. It remains this way even now, except for the moments when I stab myself with the angel's pen. Oh the blood—it is life, it is my salvation.

Gautier Ghost Story

Chad Hensley

Humid Mississippi night in mid-April
Way past late
Scratchy black woods soaked in ground fog
Slippery for miles in every direction
Thick rotten egg stench of paper mills
Almost tearing my eyes with atrophied memories.
Across milky chocolate bayou waters
In scabrous patches of clawing sea oats
Blue crab shadows whisper taunts
Below a hairline crack of jester moon.
Where choked marsh and caustic sand meet
Speckled with footprints
Drowned in deep gulf
Forgotten summers ago
I hit I-10, snarling tarmac
Trailing me for hours like rabid hound dogs,
Thin glaucous tint covering the land
Behind me.

Lucifer Romantico

Tatiana

I could feel your heart throbbing through your skin,
The world tremored with your rage;
Devils danced around us in the fire as you gently led me into the flames.
"These are the last days of Man," you said, "and here begins my reign."
You held me close as the heavens shattered with the beating of your wings.
"See my love; I cannot rest until my work is done,
I have the wrath of God burning in my veins.

"My curses will poison their minds, moving from one consciousness to
    the next.
One by one the children of Man will go mad and I will send them
marching to their deaths."

Above us the sun grew dark and died.
"Come with me," you whispered, "and reign at my side.
An era of darkness will come to be and I will reveal all to you in time."
You kissed me then and my heart became ice;
In a moment I saw eternity in your eyes.

Upon the birth of a new world to manifest,
Locked in an eternal embrace,
We will bathe in the blood of the wicked,
In a realm beyond death, love, or hate.

We Are the Owls

Jessica Amanda Salmonson

We are the owls that live underground
In a wonderful city called Knack in the Mound,
Where Andean mountain cats bear us around
To a bistro well run by a squat basset hound.
We are the owls that glide through the night
With Hecate's omens of stillbirth and blight.
Dare not to gaze on our Stygian flight;
Be not a gleam in our nocturnal sight.

You might think it funny, or something it's not,
Yet Knack in the Mound's a jocular spot.
We jest and then fall into cerebral thought,
Sipping green absinthe from far Montserrat.

Thalía

Manuel Arenas

Reposing in her bloodstained blouse
Thalía dreams of sanguine gods
Giant bats and the narrow house
Surrounded by worm-ridden clods
She ponders her appalling fate
Wondering at the remote odds
Of how she came unto this state
Between the curtain and the quick
Vexed by a thirst she cannot sate
For blood that gushes warm and slick
From riven throats that gurgle cries
Claret bubblers to lap and lick
As conscious life slips from their eyes
Each victim shudders ere he dies
Thalía smacks her lips and sighs . . .

The Wendigo

Michelle Jeffrey

Hunters, unwary, journey of their own will
To the Canadian forests, endless and still;
Two men and their guide in one small canoe
To hunt the wild moose is what they mean to do,
Paddling boldly through the swift river's gate
To the still, silent lake, lying in wait.

They set up camp with the setting sun
As the dying light of the day is done.
The guide lights the fire, the meal to make
And fog crawls over the darkening lake.
They eat quickly in silence, all ill at ease,
For they sense a presence beyond the trees.
The guide hums a dirge heavy with doubt and fear
As the Inuit do when they sense *something* near;
He starts and he stops, sniffing the air,
For he knows they're no longer alone out there.
The haunted look in his eyes makes it clear,
Slipping silently over the lake, creeping near,
Just beyond the circle of light waiting where
The darkness has swallowed the fire's brave flare.

They clutch at their guns, staying close to the fire;
Their nerves are on edge, as taunt as a wire.
Howling round the fire, the wind starts to moan,
And the name of a hunter is heard like a groan.

He screams in response and runs into the night;
His companions are stunned by his mad-seeming flight.
They call out his name, begging him to return,
And hear him cry out that his feet burn,
And his voice seems to echo from a great height
As if something was pulling him further in flight.

All through the long watches of that endless night
The others lie sleepless, frozen in fright;
But the wind returns and comes howling around,
And the voice of the lost one again seems to sound:
"Help me, my friend," and he calls him by name,
And the last hunter responds much the same.
He screams in madness and runs blindly away,
But from a far height his voice seems to say
"My feet are on fire and look how they've bled!"
The guide sits in silence, shaking his head;
He heads off in the canoe at the first light,
Leaving the damned ones to their dark plight.

Brave hunters with guns against a beast wild,
Be wary of what your sport may have riled;
For the forest has a vengeance all its own
Steeped in dark centuries of blood and bone.

She's a Legend: A Song Sung by the Unsung

John Shirley

I heard the whispers in Robber's Row—
"She is the dawn when the cock will crow;
she is the night and the firefly gleam.
She leads you through pleasure into a bad dream."
     . . . She's a legend! . . . a legend . . .
On first sight I saw a light in her eyes,
two distant candles beneath a black sky;
then the bullet of fate whistled by—
I was fortunate to be allowed to fly.
     . . . She's a legend! . . . a legend . . .
The feds found the dead across three states,
seven lonely men with identical fates;
They saw what she'd used to close their mouths:
a nightbird singing when it was daylight out.
     She's a legend! a tale told with awe by shivering men
     She's a legend! a deep dark myth without an end;
     She's a legend! Your life is a small coin she spends
     she's a legend . . . ! a legend . . .
I once asked her name, "Your real name, I mean."
"*Lilith,*" she said—a whispered scream.
"For centuries—millennia!—like rubies scattered—
I make men pay for the women they've shattered."

*   *   *

Yes the bullet of fate whistled by—
She opened her hand, *allowed* me to fly.
O she's a legend: she's an unholy grail
she let me go that I might tell the tale.
                    She's a legend!

Elegy for Futurism

Liam Garriock

The people had wanted a city, and so the aged architect had given them one. He conceived of a city of stone and iron towers, with thorny turrets and steel crenellations, of glass balconies and smooth sandstone terraces for decadent couples, steel bridges resembling arched ribcages that stretched above elevated roads where cars roved like insects, smokestacks and chimneys that belched like gigantic Bunsen burners, billboards advertising love and commerce, tunnels that yawned like the mouths of Tartarean giants, networks of motorways like arteries and veins, austere clock towers, municipal domes like gargantuan, constipated toads, mansions shaped like giant, solemn, sensual swans and peacocks, opulent ballrooms and penthouses where the most lavish orgies would take place, churches resembling snarling beasts, runic carvings carefully carved into the tessellated pavements, and basalt statues of strange and unearthly and monstrous figures in every park and courtyard.

The city was duly constructed, and, though it took a millennium to build, the architect, remarkably, lived long enough to see his vision a concrete reality. Indeed, despite being in his late eighties or early nineties, the urban planner seemed to show no sign of shuffling off this mortal coil anytime soon.

In the few weeks that passed since people began to live in the city, strange things started to occur. Lights would flicker on and off; ominous and inhuman figures would prowl the shadowy streets, watching from the corners and crevices; and outbreaks of domestic violence would occur in every neighbourhood. These soon became public, with whole crowds of strangers erupting into savage scenes of murder and perversity.

"A shudder is going through the city!" cried the people, which the papers, in all their opportunistic sensationalism, would echo. Then bodies would be found in the ancient river which girded the city, bodies with their eyes and internal organs missing, so that they were no better than broken and discarded dolls.

Blood continued to fill the streets. And soon, every machine and household appliance within the city walls began to turn on their owners, strangling and stabbing and grinding and crushing any living, organic thing. The authorities were overwhelmed with crime until they, too, succumbed to the murderous craze that spread through the city like an insidious disease. And soon, horrible figures began to appear; they could be seen crawling up the walls of glass and concrete and steel, or sometimes witnessed gnawing at the dead like ghoulish scavengers, and creatures resembling immense moths of nightmare darted through the darkening skies, snatching people off the corpse-littered ground.

The city was eventually sealed off so that the bloodthirsty plague, as the government deemed it to be, could not reach the outside world. The last man, who had a thirst for the machine that bordered on the fetishistic, tirelessly ascended the highest building in the city, a dagger in his hand. He climbed atop the metal spire and stood on its precarious surface, and, above that stricken metropolis under those tenebrous skies, passionately evoked all the gods of malice and blood and cruelty. Then he plunged the dagger into his breast in an effort to remove his heart as an offering, but he died before he could, and fell to the ground far below.

And when the city was a city of the dead, dark, empty, dismal, a modern necropolis, the aged architect stood at the bridge that once led to his creation and smiled wickedly, for he had been a devotee of the dark and mystic arts; and it was this devotion to metaphysical evil, to blood sacrifices, that saw him witness the rise and fall of cities throughout the centuries, and he could already envision the next metropolis.

Spectral Noir

Deborah L. Davitt

Cursed and sexless cynical shade,
sifting the afterlife for clues,
no mystery too great or small—
besides his own murderer's name.

Tiresias has nothing on
this gumshoe ghost, whose work brings peace
to every soul but his own, that
cursed and sexless cynical shade.

Sisyphus has it easier;
he can't remember his own name,
yet spends his whole eternity
sifting the afterlife for clues.

Strangled whores and gunned-down gangsters,
lost children left in shallow graves,
or cocoa laced with curare;
no mystery too great or small.

But no matter how he strives, both
the answer and peace elude him.
He can have everything he wants,
besides his own murderer's name.

Graveyard Feline Morning

Benjamin Blake

Walking the rows
Of aged and sunken stone
I came across a large patchwork feral cat.
Lying at its feet
Was the still, small body
Of a young rabbit.
The feline scampered away
Along the leaf-littered path
And disappeared
Into the surrounding stones.

I picked up the still-warm body
And found it still alive.
I cradled the creature in my arms,
Stroking fingers through its soft fur.

Several rows east
Sat upon the edge of a tomb
I found it had died in my hands.

I placed its limp body
Upon the grave of a dead child
Marked only with the words 'Little Tommy.'
And that's where I left it
As I wandered away
Through the crooked stones.

The Vampire's Mother

Christina Sng

She will always adore him
Even if he is now pallid and cold,
Unable to kiss her without nipping her
With his permanently extended fangs.

Each night she sits up waiting,
Worried he won't make it home.
But he always returns, mouth bloodied,
And on the front page of the next morning paper

His handiwork displayed in full color
With screaming headlines in bold sans serif:
KILLER STRIKES AGAIN
As he sleeps, curtains drawn, sound as a baby.

She becomes reclusive, unable to tell
Any of her friends why they can no longer
Come over or why she cannot meet them,
For she sleeps by day when he does.

Soon, they agree that she too should turn
As neither can live without the other.
He feeds her his blood
And gently drains her of hers

Till she sleeps
The long sleep
And awakes
An undead.

The Dark Reclaims Us

Ann K. Schwader

The dark reclaims us one by one
Within her arms, against our wills,
Unnatural children of the sun.

Reluctant to admit we're done,
We stay out late, our voices shrill
As dark reclaims us. One by one,

Doors open. Close again. What fun
Is this? Alone now, growing chilled,
Unnatural children of the sun

Without our star. This year's undone
& flapping in the branches—still
The dark reclaims us one by one

To primal silence. Sparing none,
She wraps us tight. Our time fulfilled,
Unnatural children of the sun

Drift deeper into sleep begun
With autumn & the blood it spilled
While dark reclaims us one by one,
Unnatural children of the sun.

The Unseen

Mary Krawczak Wilson

She thought she saw an oasis
In the middle of the desert.
But it was rarified red dirt—
Raining down into an abyss.

She thought she saw a small boat
On the gray horizon beyond the sea.
Was it two dark sharks—so cruel and free?
They would sink, then drown, then float.

She thought she saw a light
Through trees so high and dry.
An owl's yellowing eyes—
Burnt to cinders that night.

She thought she saw the reddened sky
Through the ethereal clouds.
But it was just a dark shroud—
Keeping her eyes closed—never to pry.

The Last God

David Barker

For two centuries the stone icon lay buried at the bottom of a pit on
ceremonial lands where it had been discarded when the people, believing
themselves modern, turned against their gods, the idols they had once
revered, and overthrew them, toppling their stern effigies, blaspheming
their sacred, unutterable names, and insulting their noble memories
with vile declarations and despicable indecencies. There, in the silence of
the soil, the icon long lay, brooding until the day when Tabor, a humble
peasant farmer, was digging a trench to irrigate his crops and struck the
stone icon with the blade of his shovel, defacing the carven god with a
score across its once-venerated visage. His discovery of the abandoned
lithic deity had long been prophesied, having been predicted by those
temple priests who, in secrecy, continued to worship in the traditional
manner after the old gods had been deposed, smashed, and cast asunder.
Thus word of what Tabor had found spread like wildfire throughout the
land, attracting many seekers who journeyed from afar, coming to the
farm to help Tabor in the task of raising the great stone image from the
pit wherein it lay. Lifting the weighty stone from the mud of the newly
exposed trench with pulleys and ropes and levers, the assembled throng
then set it upright, so that they might witness the power it still possessed
and feel the energy it yet exuded, despite the passage of 200 years
underground, out of the sight of men and women, and forgotten by all.
Standing vertical, in a position worthy of a respected god, the icon
scowled at the crowd that had gathered around it—the horde of new
believers who bowed down in supplication before its crudely chiseled
features, paying it homage during the long, hot days, praying to it
throughout the cold, star-studded nights. All who looked upon the idol's
rough, fearsome face, or turned away in terror from its hateful stare,

immediately fell prostrate upon the trembling ground, unable to bear the idol's fierce gaze, convinced of their own unworthiness in its holy presence. Thus it ruled over the kingdom wherein Tabor dwelled for several ensuing decades, a god incarnate, embodied in a coarsely worked block of volcanic stone fashioned by unknown primitives, resolute in its divinity, beyond questioning, of unchallengeable authority, until one moonless and accursed night when there approached the farm of Tabor a mob of disrespectful profligates who had swept across the land, carrying torches with which they had set ablaze the huts of countless farmers. Coming upon the ancient statue surrounded by a circle of kneeling followers, these rioters attacked, forcing the faithful to flee, then set upon the idol itself, bombarding it with rocks and spitting upon its sanctified countenance, their heretical tongues lashing the god with the vilest of oaths, mocking it, reviling it, before the ultimate indignity of pushing it over, toppling its weighty form and sending it crashing back down into the gloomy pit whence it had been excavated so long ago. With screams and howls the vandals pushed the high piles of dirt surrounding the trench back into the hole, covering the disgraced icon with mounds of earth until the stone was once again buried, as it had been when Tabor first found it that memorable day. Arising with the sun's first rays, Tabor sensed that a terrible evil had befallen his land. Running from his hut, he saw what they had done—the carven stone idol gone, the trench once more filled with dirt and rock—and he fell to his knees in grief, weeping at his misfortune, and the greater loss to his people, now that the last god was dead, slain by the least worthy among them.

Night Thoughts of a Nonentity

Manuel Pérez-Campos

Those winter-drifting abysses whose lucent
deficiencies diadem Azathoth
are rich with the convolute flux of nascent
loops and the unseen realms that rim Yuggoth.
Lo, time and space are ripe with accident
against which spells hold not, nor spectre's oath;
and as nightmares confirm I am as froth,
galaxies recede, and remain infrequent.

Even my atoms are not mine: and so when
I sense that after tempest-wracked aeons
some have been revived in unplumbed alien
forms whose inner workings appear deranged—
and that raise Yog-Sothoth through death-flumed paeans—
I feel from all allegiances to earth estranged.

When Black Tom Came

Scott J. Couturier

Old Black Tom's out rutting amid the vild stones—
ululate passion, he mates on mounds of elder bones.
That black billy-goat's tri-horned crown,
his triple-eyes, & hooves subtle as eiderdown,
his high, hypnotic, yet guttural bray
haunt these wastelands of primordial clay.

The gaunt people of the village mutter
that his displeasure sours new-churned butter—
that his third eye is a demoniacal orb
desirous of human suffering to absorb.
In fear, they leave offerings on the blighted fallow
& mutter uneasy prayers to appease & hallow.

Black Tom lures the she-goats from their pens
& impregnates them out on the reeking fens—
there, amidst menhir & shade-haunted barrow,
he cracks old bones to sup on desiccate marrow.
The kids born of Tom's abominable seed
emerge black & blood-hungry, eager to feed.

Fear consumes the village by swift degrees—
Old Black Tom, haughty three-pronged, he sees.
Hunters come to seek his hide, in vain;

they return riven, struck by fever-of-the-brain.
Finally an altar is reared of immemorial stone
& blood-offerings made with a blade of human bone.

But Old Black Tom is not yet satisfied.
Before, it was only she-goats that he plied.
On an eve of wickedly umbric Power
he bleats a beckoning to Pan's bower,
urging the women of the village to come—
& they go and copulate with him, each one.

In short order their bellies begin to swell—
the young, the old, all are infested with fell
hybrids that kick cruelly at their distorted wombs.
Out amid the groaning, bone-glutted tombs
Old Black Tom bellows his conquest lewd
while awaiting the birth of his degenerate brood.

Scholar and Sorcerer

For S. T. Joshi, on His 60th Birthday (22 June 2018)

Michael Fantina

He unrolls the scrolls from the folio there
    As the candle wick drips in the dark.
He studies his notes in that cold magic air,
The mind of a wizard to which none compare,
    While he's quick with a witty remark.

Here, hard by the sea with its slow silver foams,
    He reads over his lines once again,
Then he hefts and he thumbs through his old dusty tomes
As the moonlight creeps down in such odd burnished chromes
    While he flashes his swift agile pen.

A sorcerer he and a scholar and more,
    And is so much more than he seems.
A scholar of Edo and far Rajapur
And lost ancient cities where he's found the door
    Long lost in the realm of old dreams.

A seer of the one who knew Providence well,
    And a master of words and of lore,
The mind of a sage that's been honed by some spell,
A seer from lost stars or the Earth, none may tell!
    His aid though we ever implore!

He unrolls the scrolls from the folio there
    As the candle wick drips in the dark.
He studies his notes in that cold magic air,
The mind of a wizard to which none compare,
    While he's quick with a witty remark.

Flowers from Another World

Kendall Evans

I'd like to bring you flowers
               From another world
Write sublime poems for you
               Inspired by demons & deities
Let's have a picnic

      Beyond the boundaries of our lives
We'll invite Alice & the Mad Hatter
               Einstein & Don Juan

Maybe the White Rabbit will drop by
               Unexpectedly

Afterwards,
         I'll lick the ants off your flesh
I'll kiss your lips;
     Kiss your lovely nether lips, too
And then we will make love
               Upon the hand-crafted blanket
With its ethereal patterns, labyrinthine
               Leading us into The Mystic.

Dark Entry IV

Chad Hensley

I found a family of silverfish,
Glittery scales and caudal filaments twitching,
Living on the back cover of a magazine
Inside a white comic-book storage box.

I picked up the magazine,
But the image on the back cover crumbled
Into dusty black bits as smaller insects scurried.
I crushed the bugs beneath my fingers,
Each a tiny smeared wetness.

A very large silverfish,
Almost the size of my finger,
Bloated body glistening with a vibrant metallic hue,
Reared up on thick centipede-like hind legs.

A strange cognizance crept over me
As miniscule eye stalks on extra-long antennae
Stared at me with an ancient pity
Before I smashed the giant bug into the pages of the magazine.

But now, even hours after, my room seems smaller
And, if I listen very carefully, there is a clicking in the shadows.

The Last Illusion of Robert Houdin

Jessica Amanda Salmonson

He took off his hat, placed it on a table,
Revealing no top to his pate;
Up flew a flock of doves
To roost stage left, atop an iron gate.

He reached in his head,
Pulled out a scarf; it was red,
Attached to one that was blue
And one of brightest yellow,
Until there were one-hundred thirty-two
Colorful scarves from out of this fellow!

He took a large pitcher of milk
And poured it into his crown;
Yet when he bowed, the crowd allowed
Nothing came sluicing down.

Then standing up rigid and reaching within,
He pulled out a cavy, a hare, a meerkat,
An albino python, a large bamboo rat—
The crowd raised a praiseful din.

He pulled out a dinner plate,
Then a roast duck,
Utensils to eat it with, and, of course,
Mead in a mug. What luck!

The crowd was in thrall when last of all
With dramatic flourish he held forth his brain,
Then fell to the floor to the orchestra's score,
Never to rise up again.

On Wings of Fire

David B. Harrington

The mystic meditates lazily beneath a shady fruit tree and envisions spiritual enlightenment, his key to achieving inner peace.

Through a kaleidoscope of colors that spin before his eyes, he sees the Seven Riders of the Rainbow in their horse-drawn chariots blaze a trail of fire across the spiritual sky. And closing his eyes, he traces their path with his finger.

Ever so gently he reaches up and plucks a virtuous fruit, careful not to disturb the serpent who lies basking in the midday sun. But Cherubim watch over the garden with their flaming swords and guide the seer on his mystical journey through the Land of Shadows and spiritual darkness, where evil lurks behind every hidden doorway.

So taking a bite, the mystic's eyes open wide and he sees a fleet of wooden ships sailing smoothly across a crystal sea, like white swans gliding gracefully upon a lotus-filled pond.

He is strolling down a winding road now, through a lush rainforest covered in moss and evergreen, where primeval giants tower high above his head.

Onward through the meadows he wanders, past fountains and streams where nymphs and gnomes, efts and olms frolic on frosted fields, and hummingbirds are busy collecting sweet nectar from a honeysuckle bush. Where the first morning dew clings softly to silk-spun webs and fuzzy caterpillars hatch into beautiful living butterflies.

It's evening now and the long tall shadows of the late afternoon slowly disappear into the fading light. The mystic rests his tired feet on an old hollow log and listens to the nightbird call.

A hoot owl screeches somewhere off in the distance, wolves and coyotes bay at the full moon, and the wild wind howls down the canyon.

The dragon awakens like some legendary mythical creature in a lost and forgotten story of old. The dragon's breath closes in on the seer now, surrounding him in a shroud of mist.

But through the haze he sees the golden hawk with its great wings of fire descending through the twelve solar gates, and it perches upon his outstretched hand.

So he plucks a feather from each of its wings: Now he has the magic power at his fingertips and he soars majestically off into the spiritual sky.

The Merman

Tatiana

Oh, how your cheeks reddened and your eyes gleamed,
Like dancing flames reflected on the night sea,
Off the coast of Venice.

How I yearned for you to be close, but the sins past could not be done;
True love is unconditional—all else is illusion.

The merman swims against the tide,
He delves into the depths of my mind,
Pulling me deep into the sea,
Stealing what is left of me.

A trail of black hearts left under the flowers you crushed,
Your love has grown cold—as cold as your blood;
You trussed up my thoughts, drowned me in misery,
You lured me into your arms and dragged me deep into the sea,

    Swimming against the tide,
    Into the depths of my mind,
    Pulling me deep into the sea,
    Stealing what's left of me.

My thoughts are shrouded in the shadows of a dream
As the day wrenches me from this;
I feel your kiss slipping away from me, fading away from me,
Into the watery abyss.

Of Hooves and Horns

Michelle Jeffrey

Within the depths of velvet forest
Something stirs
Elusive scent lichen and moss
Ferns and firs
Movement slight scarcely seen
Rarely caught
Shadows move the darkness dancing
Edge of thought
Wilderness walking stalking shadow
Soft sounding
Hooves clatter striking stone
Wild bounding
Taunting glimpse horned shadow
Falling light
Calling drawing through the veil
Darkness bright

Weird Tales, the First Run: An Homage

Frank Coffman

The pages now are yellowing to rust—
Aged issues of "The Unique Magazine."
And most who wrote for it have long been dust.
Yet, though they've passed, as every artist must,
Their words live on, fly forth and still careen
Off later minds. Those wildly-written pages—
Some for all Time, some to fall between
The spaces in Fame's net, not to be seen
By many with the passing of the Ages.
Each month the weirding verses and strange tales
From the rich mix of "also-wrotes" and sages
Went forth. And still their strange quill-work engages
Us, enthralled by their magic that prevails—
Lives on until the lust for Wonder fails.

[A "Revbaiyat" Sonnet (see p. 24 of this issue).]

In Ligno

Deborah L. Davitt

Under the boughs, shadows darkle—
from each bole, barkish faces leer,
trees lift their limbs to the sky,
branches laden with dark leaves.

Shade pools beneath them,
fitting hollows, filling earthen curves
where graves lie, untended—
no wreaths left here;
just the teeth of cheatgrass
and the malice of starthistle.

Not far from the hidden graves,
stones protrude from the ground—
a ruined foundation became a tombstone
for a house, formed from its own bones.

Sometimes teenagers come here
on a dare or a date,
for the delicious rush of fear
that heightens their senses
better than any drug.

The leaves whisper old tales to them,
of feuding families;
of gunshots traded at saloons,

of bullets fired through windows
of stone-walled houses, like this one.

They rustle a story of how love grew
like a tree's spreading branches,
between the daughter of one rancher,
the son of another;

of how, when he joined an attack
led by his father and brothers,
he fired wide, just to divert suspicion
from his allegiances;

of how the bullet flew astray,
how it bounced off that stone wall—
how it deflected through her heart.

Of how he shot himself at
her funeral, with the same gun.

Delicious, delicious, sweet sorrow,
the wind in the leaves susurrates.

And among the hollows,
in the pools of shadow,
young lovers roll together,

feeling the surge of ancient anguish,
the teeth of cheatgrass biting their flesh like bullets,
a familiar rage against parental stupidity,
and gut-knotting defiance—

Then clinging together, desperately,
feeling more for each other now
than ever before, as a storm breaks
through the branches, voices howling from the gale.
Don't forget, never forget—

But in dawn's gray light
they stumble back to their cars,
wondering how it was
that they ever took it that far,
that he said *I love you*,
that she said, I give myself to you.

And puzzled, they can't meet each other's eyes
as the leaves whisper
sad farewells.

The Mermaid

Christina Sng

Once I dreamed
Of my days of youth
When I walked
On shores with sand.

I fell in love
With a haunting song
And the face
That came along.

How we loved
Like siren gods
Till he killed me
With a nod.

They threw me back
Into the guileless sea,
Limbless
And reborn.

She took my voice
And she took my soul
As I traded them
For revenge.

The scythe I swung
Curved beautifully,
Leaving arcs
Of the crescent moon.

I gave his head
To the old sea witch
Who happily
Completed the spell.

Now I walk
With human skin
And two strong legs,
Free as the wind.

I miss my tail,
But not as much
As the forgotten depths
Of my human soul.

When Nightfall Comes to Ooth-Nargai

A Reverie after Reading H. P. Lovecraft's "Celephaïs"

Manuel Pérez-Campos

The snowmelt-tumulted bourne, in its boulder-
slamm'd leaps, is multiplying the alienness
of first stars through stray'd drops on Kuranes'
tilted walking stick: and as he grows colder

and feels his joints practicing to be dead,
he mulls, beneath an afreet-visag'd mist,
that having aeons in which to exist
and voids without end is the norm o'erhead

until the earthbound tenet of remaining
circumscrib'd seems odd: it is here he keeps
vigil by ruins to get reacquainted

with wanderlust, and to be comforted
by Celephaïs afar; and to dream of deeps,
and of regaining the aim of unknowing.

The Autumn Sphinx

Liam Garriock

I love the darker evenings when autumn and winter rule over the earth. I love those quiet nights, those windy evenings, when darkness is ubiquitous, when gloom is around every corner, and lampposts illuminate the empty streets. What manner of people hurry on home through the dark? Schoolgirls amazed at the darkness, marching thugs, solemn loners . . .

I walked through the park once on a late and deadening November afternoon, carrying a great burden upon me. The shadows were everywhere, and they followed me. The whole world was swiftly being encased in the great and sombre November gloom, which encroaches upon the world like a black wave. And here we all were, walking on to our dwellings in the caliginous cavities of that unconquerable Sphinx of autumn, my heart and my thoughts darkened by other things that the Sphinx took no heed of. Darkness, too dark even to see the dead leaves that lie scattered on the ground.

I would wait by the water, watching the calm and restless cedar sea, and the grey clouds blindly hover to the city and above its busy streets. Everyone else had their duties; the fishmongers cut open dead fish, the school children studied and walked on home, men with briefcases walked all the way from work or on the buses, but I was as a ghost trapped among the living, a wanderer without purpose or aim.

The Sphinx has returned, for now is its time of year. Its paws rest on every corner of the city, and its cold breath whispers through the lonely streets. Its food is the mortal sun and the melancholy of visionaries, and it hungrily devours the transient daylight outside and belches out and defecates the darkness and gloom we all despise; but darkness and gloom breed strange things. The marriage of solemn enchantment and autumnal melancholy remains a potent alchemy. Wonder, romance, mystery . . . bitterness . . . The Sphinx is the father and the mother of all dreams.

Classic Reprints

The Creaking Door

Madison Cawein

Come in, old Ghost of all that used to be!—
    You find me old,
    And love grown cold,
And fortune fled to younger company:
Departed, as the glory of the day,
With friends!—And you, it seems, have come to stay.—
    'Tis time to pray.

Come; sit with me, here at Life's creaking door,
    All comfortless.—
    Think, nay! then, guess,
What was the one thing, he? that made me poor?—
The love of beauty, that I could not bind?
My dream of truth? or faith in humankind?—
    But, never mind!

All are departed now, with love and youth,
    Whose stay was brief;
    And left but grief
And gray regret—two jades, who tell the truth;—
Whose children—memories of things to be,
And things that failed,—within my heart, ah me!
    Cry constantly.

None can turn time back, and no man delay
    Death when he knocks.—
    What good are clocks,
Or human hearts, to stay for us that day
When at Life's creaking door we see his smile,—
Death's! at the door of this old House of Trial?—
    Old Ghost, let's wait awhile.

[From Cawein's *The Cup of Comus: Fact and Fancy* (New York: Cameo Press, 1915).]

The Fairy Changeling

Dora Sigerson Shorter

Brian O'Byrne of Omah town
In his garden strode up and down;
He pulled his beard, and he beat his breast;
And this is his trouble and woe confessed:

"The good-folk came in the night, and they
Have stolen my bonny wean away;
Have put in his place a changeling,
A weashy, weakly, wizen thing!

"From the speckled hen nine eggs I stole,
And lighting a fire of a glowing coal,
I fried the shells, and I spilt the yolk;
But never a word the stranger spoke.

"A bar of metal I heated red
To frighten the fairy from its bed,
To put in the place of this fretting wean
My own bright beautiful boy again.

"But my wife had hidden it in her arms,
And cried, 'For shame!' on my fairy charms;
She sobs, with the strange child on her breast;
'I love the weak, wee babe the best!'"

To Bryan O'Byrne's, the tale to hear,
The neighbours came from far and near:
Outside his gate, in the long boreen,
They crossed themselves, and said between

Their muttered prayers, "He has no luck!
For sure the woman is fairy-struck,
To leave her child a fairy guest,
And love the weak, wee wean the best!"

[From Shorter's *Collected Poems* (London: Hodder & Stoughton, 1907).]

Articles

Clark Ashton Smith and Robert Nelson: Master and Apprentice: Part 1

Marcos Legaria

In July 1934, Robert Nelson (1912–1935), a budding young writer of St. Charles, Illinois, wrote to the poet, short fiction writer, and artist Clark Ashton Smith (1893–1961) of Auburn, California, regarding Smith's appreciation of Nelson's poem "Below the Phosphor" which had appeared in Charles D. Hornig's *Fantasy Fan* for June 1934:

> Thanks for your good word on *Below The Phosphor*. This was written in 1928, and is simple, mimetic. However, just before I sent it to Hornig, I endeavored to make the poem 'scan' as well as possible, and changed wording slightly from the original. I wish to think of it as only a miscellaneous poem of mine.[1]

"Below the Phosphor" seems to be an early poem in Nelson's oeuvre, and so his assessment of it is perhaps a bit harsh. The poem does bear some traces of the content and style of Edgar Allan Poe and deserves to be quoted in full:

> The swaying corpse upon the wall
> Grows rotten with the waning light;

---

1. Nelson, letter to Smith (6 July 1934); ms., John Hay Library, Brown University (hereafter abbreviated JHL).

And crawling shadows of the night
Lie on the body like a pall.

Dead spirits dance upon the slope;
Blatant are bat-things overhead;
But now the revenants have fled,
The glad fantasias yet grope.

Only the ghouls are gently stirred
By tainted gusts lost from the gale;
And in the faun-infested vale
Wild screeches of a fiend are heard.

Impending o'er the noisome spawn,
In glaucous haze the Phosphor steals—
Thence to Azrael's eyes reveals
The wrestling wraiths on death's dark lawn—

Fast scaling up the ebon sky
To cull and slay the gnawing blight,
All cool of the corpse's mute delight,
Or if the baneful fiend should die.

Because the influence of Poe was evident among Nelson's early poems, Smith had suggested that Nelson seek out Poe's essays and "Marginalia," and Nelson eagerly complied:

> Many, many thanks for your suggestion that I read Poe's "The Philosophy of Composition." I read it carefully, and I read his "Letter to Mr. B——," "The Poetic Principle," and I am now reading his "The Rationale of Verse." I only wish I had read these long ago. They will help me tremendously.[2]

Nelson also revealed to Smith his own method of composition, perhaps a bit sarcastically but sincerely:

> All of my writing is done in longhand first, for I wish to pace the floor and tear up my hair. This is a gross exaggeration. At times, my room is not

---

2. Nelson, letter to Smith (24 April 1934); ms., JHL.

large enough to hold me, and very often I am literally forced to abandon it and take a long walk along the river (not far away from my home) or else sit alone in the woods and watch and listen to the birds.[3]

A year after he wrote "Below the Phosphor," Nelson read for the first time a copy of *Weird Tales* (October 1929).[4] In editor Farnsworth Wright's obituary for Nelson (d. 22 July 1935) in *Weird Tales* of November 1935, he drew attention to Nelson's tutelage under Clark Ashton Smith:

> [. . .] Robert Nelson [. . .] had developed a deep poetic feeling and a keen sensitivity to the overtones and undertones of words, which made his verse stand out boldly from among the average magazine poetry. He received his first encouragement from no less a poet than Clark Ashton Smith himself. His work gave clear promise that he would some day occupy an important place among the great poets; a promise that now—alas!—can never be fulfilled.

Under Smith's guidance, and to a lesser extent Wright's, Nelson's entrance into *Weird Tales* would be his poem "Sable Revery" (September 1934). Nelson composed the initial draft in December 1933 and January 1934. He had previously written a sketch in praise of Smith's "The Double Shadow" and "The Weird Tale (A Dialogue)," in November 1933, slated to appear in the May 1934 issue of the *Fantasy Fan*.[5] Since "Sable Revery" is the focus of this essay, it is presented in its entirety below:

> Black roses sprout across the sky,
> Pipes sing insensate 'neath the sea,
> The clamant heads of madmen fly
> And shatter with a dark outcry,
> As tones transpose to deeper dye
> And leaves whirl wild with jubilee
> Through the mad organist's rambling brain;
> In the disordered sepulcher

---

3. Nelson, letter to Smith (14 July 1934); ms., JHL.
4. Nelson, letter to Smith (5 June 1934); ms., JHL.
5. Nelson, letter to Smith (24 April 1934); ms., JHL.

A lady's dead eyes strive to stir,
She dares to laugh, but all in vain;
Three-fingered hands paint a far frieze
With the black blood of vanquished devils,
Who sway and slay the music-breeze
In their daft and dying revels.

Now ebon fluids 'gin to flow
And drip with waxen candle-men;
Black disks of stone are trundling low;
From the organ's bosom fuming slow,
Fouler and sadder perfumes blow
To drown the bournes of demon ken;
Skulls flown from swarthy corpses kiss
And feed upon the organist's soul,
Which ne'er doth cease to toll and toll
Bell-like within this dusk abyss;
Fell plants and flowers writhe in wombs
Of blighted worlds remote from the morn,
And musty myrrh exhales from tombs
Whirling in utmost stars forlorn.

Swart suns on sounding waters swell
The turgid notes to direr din,
And murky spirits soar from hell
To flap their cerements palpable
In the wild player's face, and tell
Jet jewels into his mouth, and spin
Mad gossamers amid his hair;
Swift raven locks entwine his throat,
His eyes no longer glare and gloat;
As from a tower high in air,
The console wakes a weirder fear;
His flaming, fitful fingers chill;
One tear he weeps, a dead man's tear:
The sable revery is still.

The line "Swift raven locks entwine his throat" indicates that Nelson was already suffering from tuberculosis when he composed the poem.

Smith's influence on Nelson began with Nelson's acquisition of Smith's *Ebony and Crystal*,[6] and his reading of Smith's poetry in *Weird Tales* and the *Fantasy Fan*. Nelson shares his feelings about Smith's poetry in a letter he wrote to Smith dated 27 March 1934, enclosing a line from "Ode to the West Wind" by Percy Bysshe Shelley, who had also passed away at a young age:

> I was greatly surprised to see a poem of such high excellence as your *Revenant*, appearing in the March issue of Fantasy Fan. Truly it has all of that immortal beauty that one finds in *Ebony and Crystal* and is like the music swept from that "wild harp of time," which Shelley performed upon the world's ear with eternal melody.[7]

In January 1934, visited Wright at the offices of *Weird Tales* bringing his draft of "Sable Reverie." Wright described this encounter in a letter to Smith:

> Robert Nelson was in the WEIRD TALES office several weeks ago, and I saw SABLE REVERIE then—undoubtedly before you had seen it. Mr. Nelson offered to tear it up if I did not think it had possibilities, but I vetoed the suggestion at once. I did not give him any constructive criticism of the poem, except to point out that he had much faulty rhythm in the poem, and that some of his imagery was hard to understand. [. . .] Nelson is still a youth on the sunny side of twenty, but his imagination struck me as having great possibilities.[8]

Wright's letter was a reply to Smith's dated 26 February, in which Smith had praised "Sable Reverie," having read it not long after Wright did. Nelson sheds some light on what Smith told Wright on 8 March 1934:

> Wright showed me your letter to him commending Sable Reverie, and, in fact, gave me the letter to keep. I do not know how I could ever repay you in appreciation for what you have done for me, Mr. Smith. I know that

---

6. Nelson, letter to Smith (14 April 1934); ms., JHL.

7. Nelson, letter to Smith (27 March 1934); ms., JHL.

8. Wright, letter to Smith (1 March 1934), ms., JHL.

your letter to Wright had tremendous weight in bringing my poem to its now insured and inevitable acceptance for publication in Weird Tales. Thanks a *thousandfold*.[9]

Nelson had written to Smith on 21 February 1934 of his meeting with Wright: "Only in my first interview with Wright we were talking of you and your work, and it is needless for me to say that his opinion of you was of the highest."[10] Following that meeting, Nelson and Smith corresponded regularly. In late January 1934, Nelson sent Smith a revised version of "Sable Reverie." Smith surprised Nelson with more than just a response. A sense of Smith's generosity toward Nelson can be gained from Nelson's reply to Smith:

> This can only be the beginning in thanking you for your greatly helpful and thorough going criticisms and suggestions regarding my poem. I am certainly happy that you did not find it wholly disappointing.
>
> I readily see that I had sketched only an ambiguous, discordant outline. But now you have come along with your own easel and painting materials—and what a transformation: And what am I to say? I spent the whole of last night reading and rereading your letter and your typed copy of my poem in the last stanza, especially you transfigured my imagery[11] into something *glowingly* beautiful: It is something which I myself fear to retouch again. Your other revisions I may change. For instance I may say, "Three-fingered hands *paint* a far frieze." And "To drown and maim all demon ken." And "Great disks of black stone trundle low." My "waxen candle-men" I did not evolve from thoughts about the ancient wizards. The whole poem, of course, I had tried to write as if I were the very organist himself, endeavoring to sleep myself within a darksome, maddening reverie, with the knowing or unknowing resultant conclusion that my mind would

---

9. Nelson, letter to Smith (8 March 1934); ms., JHL.

10. Nelson, letter to Smith (21 February 1934); ms., JHL.

11. This was one of the weaknesses that Wright found in "Sable Reverie," as pointed out to Smith in his 1 March 1934 communication: "[S]ome of his imagery was hard to understand" (JHL). Nelson shortly explains to Smith how the poem's vagueness came into play.

forever be tossing in its unresting sea. That is why, perhaps, you noted the 'certain harshness, the vague and blurred imagery.'[12]

One of the passions in Nelson's life and how it laid the background to "Sable Revery" pours forth:

> I have spent over eight years in the intensive study of music and love it, perhaps, more than ever I could adore a painting, statue, or even a woman. Although I have known many species of the latter, I generally avoid and shun them, and all the more since an unhappy experience with one. But wondrous music is ever my *true* lover, always ready to take me in its soul-caressing arms. It never betrays, never violates one's heart.[13]

Once Nelson had revised the poem, he suggested that Smith might in a good word for him with Farnsworth Wright to secure the poem a berth in *Weird Tales*:

> But now let me say again how much I value your criticism, suggestions, and your own admiration for my poem. And if you could or would recommend it to Wright I am almost sure it would carry weight. Oh, it must! [. . .] I really feel so appreciative of your aid that I am literally forced to say that, at the moment, I should gladly climb past the highest pinnacle, and step through the very windows of heaven, and far beyond. Such is my appreciation.[14]

Nelson visited Wright a second time on 8 March 8 1934, bring his revised "Sable Reverie." Wright accepted the poem but not until Nelson corrected some faulty scansion:

> "And leaves whirl in wild jubilee" and the other, "Great disks of black stone trundle low." He thought that the long stress on "in" after the short stress on "whirl" didn't swing so well with the rest of the line. And the same with "black" and "stone" of the other line. For revision I have thought: "And leaves whirl wild in jubilee" and "Black disks of stone are trundling low." These two should remedy it all I think. At the moment I am also sending these two revised lines to Wright, together with a retyped

---

12. Nelson, letter to Smith (21 February 1934); ms., JHL.
13. Ibid.
14. Ibid.

manuscript of the poem to see what he thinks of it this time. I will let you
know, of course, when and if he accepts the poem finally this time, which I
surely hope he will. As I inferred, he will take the poem as soon as the
aforementioned lines are revised a bit and meets his final approval.[15]

Nelson later notified Smith of yet an additional revision: "Just before I
sent S.R. to Wright I changed 'leaves whirl with jubilee' instead of 'in.'
This might be better. I'll let you know W's final verdict."[16]

The alterations proved beneficial. Nelson wrote to Smith about
Wright's acceptance of "Sable Reverie" and acknowledged Wright's and
Smith's aid:

> Sable Reverie has been definitely accepted by Mr. Wright for
> publication in Weird Tales. I just received word of this in my morning
> mail.
>
> The two revised lines, Wright said improved greatly the poem. The
> lines now are: "And leaves whirling wild with jubilee" instead of the
> former. "And leaves whirl in wild jubilee," and "Black disks of stone are
> trundling low" in lieu of the former, "Great disks of black stone trundle
> low." The line you suggested "To drown the bournes of demon ken," I
> employed. Thanks. [. . .] As you have said, he certainly (Wright) has his own
> ideas: However, I think his ideas for revising the 2 lines of my poem were
> keen and for the best. Aside from his rigid, individual opinions of writers
> and literature and life, in general, I have the greatest respect for him.
>
> But please accept again, Mr. Smith, my deepest appreciation for you
> kindness and time in reading Sable Reverie, giving your greatly wonderful
> suggestions for revision and alterations in meter, and your letter of praise to
> Farnsworth Wright. Please know that all of this has meant a great deal to
> me. Yet, too, I realize that you would have never done all of this had not
> my poem itself possessed the substance and inspiration that it did and does.
> [. . .] But lastly, in view of what I have just finished saying, I owe everything
> to *you*, whom so much is due in bringing Sable Reverie to its final *perfection*
> and acceptance.[17]

---

15. Nelson, letter to Smith (8 March 1934); ms., JHL.
16. Nelson, postcard to Smith [postmarked 8 March 1934]; ms., JHL.
17. Nelson, letter to Smith (12 March 1934); ms., JHL.

At the time Nelson wrote to Smith on 11 May 1934, the title of "Sable Reverie" had been changed to "Sable Revery,"[18] probably by Wright.

Nelson's sincere admiration of and indebtedness to Smith are evident in Nelson's letters. A dichotomy can be pointed out in Nelson's "Sable Revery," where a rare glimpse can be viewed into his original version of the poem, as evinced in this essay before Smith's and Wright's contributions. Nelson's final vision of the poem blended with those enhancements of Smith's and Wright's. Nelson the apprentice dutifully applied the insights offered by Smith and Wright.

Nelson's humility toward Smith is apparent at the end of his second letter to Smith, dated 8 March 1934, and the apprenticeship he enlisted himself into led him on a path to a hopeful but short future:

> I enclose a stamp just in case you wish to answer this letter. I really do not wish to become too much of a pest or burden to you in any way. But I really consider you my Master and I am willing to *follow*. [. . .] I have completed a poem entitled Dream-Stair and am working on another. [19] These poems I have tried to make as 'different' and macabre as possible. However, I realize *this* sort of thing can also be a bit overdone: yet I have endeavored to present them as 'logically' as it is possible. I'd like to send them to you just to see what you think of their possibilities.[20]

A dark storm would make its way into the horizon of Nelson's and Smith's correspondence, as Nelson reiterated: "I hope I didn't prove too personal or boyishly flagrant concerning myself in my last letter. I am given too many moods, and my prevailing spirits are apt to alter immediately and many times. You must forgive me."[21]

18. Nelson, letter to Smith (11 May 1934); ms., JHL.

19. Robert Nelson, "Under the Tomb," *Weird Tales* 23, No. 5 (May 1934): 581.

20. Nelson, letter to Smith (8 March 1934); ms., JHL.

21. Nelson, letter to Smith (19 March 1934), ms., JHL.

Reviews

In the Footsteps of the Masters

Donald Sidney-Fryer

HENRY J. VESTER III. *Of Mist and Crystal: Selected Poetry.* Fungoid Press/VirtualBookworm.com Press, 2015. 74 pp. $16.96 hc.

It is obvious that poet Henry J. Vester III is at least a literary connoisseur, as his hardcover book of poetry reveals the lore and appreciation of the modern masters of prose and poetry in the genre(s) of literature involving a general fantasy and science-fiction perspective, as the poet himself reveals in his "Author's Forward" [*sic*]: H. P. Lovecraft, Robert E. Howard, George Sterling, Joseph Payne Brennan, Stanley McNail, Ambrose Bierce, Richard L. Tierney, Ann K. Schwader, and (above all) Clark Ashton Smith, otherwise Klarkash-Ton. The author himself bears witness that he nourished his first tastes in poetry (apart from, but including, E. A. Poe) on the following volumes: *Dark of the Moon,* the anthology of weird and macabre poetry edited by August Derleth (1947); the later and similar volume *Fire and Sleet and Candlelight,* also edited by Derleth (1961); and the *Collected Poems* of H. P. Lovecraft, likewise edited by Derleth (1963). The anthologist-editor published all three volumes through his publishing firm Arkham House (Sauk City, Wisconsin). The present volume has two appreciative and exceptional introductions, the first by W. H. Pugmire, the second by Gregorio Montejo. Henry Vester well deserves the praise and elucidation, the lore and learning, imparted by these introductions.

This first book of poetry, and also the author's first solo volume of any type, is a small handsome hardcover, a little gem of production (5.25

× 8.25″), with a handsome cover by Allen Koszowski, a practiced artist of the weird and fantastic. In addition to the three prefaces, the volume contains twenty-four poems in verse and ends with a poem in prose, as well as with "Some Notes on the Poems" (these are helpful) assembled by the poet himself—explaining and identifying people and places in a playful manner. The back cover gives us basic information "About the Author," now a retired social worker who has worked as a family therapist near or at Santa Rosa, California, but most recently in a large community mental health center at Klamath Falls, Oregon.

Mr. Vester writes in variety of styles and forms whether traditional or non-traditional, clearly and straightforwardly. As noted by Gregorio Montejo, he commands "a dark yet sinuous line," no less than a broad range of imagery and allusion, both of which come to the fore in the tributes to various poetic masters. Chilling moments abound in the poems themselves, but succinctly, as in the poetry of Ambrose Bierce and Leah Bodine Drake. (Relative to some hunters who go exploring where they should not, "In the tower was horrible laughter.")

The poet first strikes the note of lonely and macabre reflection in the opening morceau, "Medicine Wind," and sustains it throughout all nine stanzas:

> I sat this eve alone
> In an unfrequented place,
> Disdaining solace or companion
> In the hour of my reflection.

He has also mastered a subtle allusiveness as presented in the poem's second stanza, where he refers to the sun and the moon respectively:

> And as the desert's master
> Drowned himself again in bloodied sands,
> Its mistress arose in haste,
> As a lover tardy to a secret tryst.

The final two stanzas resume the poem's metaphysical depths in an expert way:

All through the night the song went on,
Oblivious of any ear.
And all the threads of my spirit
It untangled, reweaving in its own image.

And as the master rose again,
I suddenly remembered, and
The spirit wind flew, laughing, away,
Salting again my bones with sandy tears.

Mixed in with all the macabre reflections, often with startling surprise endings, Mr. Vester reveals a very nice sense of humor, as in one of the tributes to H. P. Lovecraft, "An Old Gentleman Seeks Professional Help." The tribute to pictorial artist Gervasio Gallardo, "Visionary," is no less notable in its precise and serious register of the covers that Gallardo painted for Ballantine's Adult Fantasy series. The poet proves again his sense of humor in "A Yuletide Encounter," where he does an adroit and clever take-off of "A Visit from St. Nicholas," otherwise "The Night Before Christmas," and to hilarious effect. Other tributes to Lovecraft appear in "The Bells of R'lyeh," "Dagon's Halls," and "The Scroll of Alhazred." Mr. Vester strikes perhaps his deepest notes or tones in the tributes to Clark Ashton Smith, "To the Shade of Klarkash-Ton" and "Klarkash-Ton Walks at Midnight." In the first cited poem Vester's use of the true second person singular seems especially appropriate and moving. The second piece of homage turns out just as lovely and serious, a touching *jeu d'esprit*.

We can point to other titles and tributes, notably the one to "Ray" (the master fantaisiste Ray Bradbury), but rather than that, and further quotations from Mr. Vester's poetry, we would urge the serious reader to obtain a copy of *Of Mist and Crystal* and con the poems' individual morceaux. Altogether then, we can heartily recommend this book, this unequivocally delectable book, to the literary connoisseur and lover of imaginary poetry. And we have almost forgotten to add that the concluding prose-poem, "Of Ancient Glory" (4.5 pp.), is a rare and profoundly moving work of art worthy of Lord Dunsany and Ashton Smith!

One final note. The author in his preface lists various poets and other writers who have influenced and liberated his poetic vision, his inner landscape of dream and revery. We repeat them here: Edgar Allen Poe, H. P. Lovecraft, Robert E. Howard, George Sterling, Joseph Payne Brennan, Stanley McNail, Ambrose Bierce, Richard L. Tierney, Ann K. Schwader, and Clark Ashton Smith (shades of Poe and Sterling intensified!), and probably others as well (but unregistered). This quality is something that he shares with C. Ashton Smith. It relates to something fundamental to style (or subject), and that remains the *tone* of the language carefully sifted and selected by the poet (Vester), a quality as impeccable as Ashton Smith's own, or (in French) that of Baudelaire. On those grounds alone Henry Vester finds himself among the modern elect as registered by himself.

We cannot resist quoting in full one more poem, or so.

ECHOES

Echoes of a winter wind
Whisper within an ancient skull—

Stir memories of loves long lost,
The more hungered for because
They never were.

AWAKE

Who treads so softly 'round
That none but ghosts of bats in attic dark
Discern the steps which scarcely tramp the snow?
I lie awake by single candle's glow,
And dare not sleep for fear of that
Which unprotected dreams may show.

A New Formalist

Frank Coffman

ASHLEY DIOSES. *Diary of a Sorceress*. New York: Hippocampus Press, 2017. 170 pp. $15.00 tpb.

Ashley Dioses's name and reputation as a poet are not new with the publication of this tome, collecting more than 80 of her offerings in verse. Her work has appeared in many speculative journals and anthologies in recent years. This review can only hope to sketch an outline of the nature, variety, poetic modes, and quality of her work.

Published by Hippocampus Press, which has become a justly honored and widely recognized house for the preservation of old standards in speculative, horrific, and fantastic genres and the publication of the work of more contemporary authors and poets, the book is in normal trade paperback format with a full-color photograph front cover and several black and white interior illustrations.

The book contains an introduction by master bard Donald Sidney-Fryer, who remarks:

> These lapidary selections reveal a practiced auctorial hand and a keen and enshadowed imagination. The poet-author has already gained an enviable and hard-earned reputation for herself via the many appearances of her poems in various magazines especially devoted to fantasy and the macabre.

Following a prelude poem, "My Dark Diary," Dioses divides the "diary" into sections: "Entry One: Atop the Crystal Moon"; "Entry Two: Kiss the Stars"; "Entry Three: Star Lightning"; and "Entry Four: On a Dreamland's Moon." In each section, a poem by the same title is included. There is a short section of "Tributes" to the poet following these sections.

Ashley Dioses is a "New Formalist" in that she is both relatively "new" and certainly a "formalist," practicing the traditional modes of verse, using both meter and rhyme. Having said that, her work shows several influences from "Old Formalists"—especially those in the Bohemian Californian tradition of George Sterling, Clark Ashton

Smith, and Donald Sidney-Fryer; but also the poets prominent in the early incarnation of *Weird Tales* in the 1920s and '30s: H. P. Lovecraft, Robert E. Howard, and, again, Smith (and possibly Donald Wandrei).

Many of her verses are self-expressive lyrics, making use of several traditional forms and some fixed forms such as the sonnet and the rondel. She also works with descriptive narratives, one exceptional example being "Witch Lord of the Hunt," done in hexameter quatrains and displaying a keen ability for creating vivid imagery. Two influences upon her poetry are clear in her longer homage poem "Atop the Crystal Moon," which shows—as her dedicatory parenthesis under the title would indicate—the influence of both George Sterling and his important poem, "A Wine of Wizardry," and also of Clark Ashton Smith and his equally important *The Hashish-Eater* (Smith himself was the protégé of and inspired by Sterling). Her poem is set in iambic pentameters with random but clearly echoed rhyme, very much like Sterling's technique in his poem.

Many of her poems are solidly descriptive in emphasis, even if narrative in nature, and she makes use of ballad-like quatrain stanzas in several places, with a few in very short lines of iambic trimeter—even briefer than the standard ballad form.

An excellent variant sonnet is the poem, "Selkie," based upon the legend of that creature's ability to remove her pelt and become a woman rather than a seal, but subject to being captured and held as a woman if the pelt is hidden. The sonnet shows a blend of Italian and English forms, clearly demonstrating the poet's willingness—while chiefly writing in the "box" of tradition—to break out of the "box" in poetic experimentation.

There is an excellent example of *topographia* (description of a place) in "The Abandoned Garden," fine use of the ballad stanza in her tribute to Nora May French, "The Perfect Rose," and, again, a familiarity with a variety of traditions in using Shakespeare's Venus and Adonis stanza for "Graveyard Blossom."

Several poems are clearly lyrics to Ms. Dioses's "significant other" and fellow accomplished poet, K. A. Opperman. These include work with the fixed French form of the Rondel. Many of her poems are quite brief—four to eight lines. This, perhaps, shows some influence from Emily Dickinson and her tight, short, ballad-like quatrains.

In a sort of blend of the bucolic and the ballad, the poem "Panic" touches upon the two myths regarding the little satyr-god: one, the ushering in of spring, playing the reed-pipes and prancing about to help Nature's rebirth; the second, the encountering of him that causes "panic"—derived, of course from his name.

Another favorite subject is Countess Bathory, famous for allegedly ordering the killing of young maidens and then bathing in their blood in order, so she believed, to perpetuate her youth. Several of the poems commingle the horrific with the erotic, somewhat like the sonnet works of Park Barnitz.

This reviewer was not as enamored of the interior illustrative works as of the poetry. The one facing "Witch Lord of the Hunt" is well wrought, but some others, while, of course, not detracting from the overall quality of the poetry, are not on a par with it.

All in all, Dioses's poetry shows a fine sense of meter and rhythm and an aptness for finding the right rhyme. *Diary of a Sorceress* does a good job of covering a variety of modes, moods, and methods. Her poetry is traditionally inspired, yet interestingly fresh. It is definitely a recommended read for any interested in speculative poetics and its current state.

Drowning in Delicious Weird

Russ Parkhurst

ADAM BOLIVAR. *The Lay of Old Hex: Spectral Ballads & Weird Jack Tales*. New York: Hippocampus Press, 2017. 327 pp. $20.00 tpb.

The Lay of Old Hex is a compendium and in places a melding of two major forms of storytelling, poesy and prosody. Both forms are as old as human time, and even when one considers some of the more recent literary antecedents for Mr. Bolivar's work we find that in common with the best writers in literature he is essentially a storyteller. The stories he tells reach back to some of our earliest cultural memories when we gathered 'round the fire at night, whispered our wonder of common events, and enchanted our young with fairy tales. Centuries later, when oral storytelling was the only book in town, we bandied street ballads about in taverns and sang the work of Coleridge and Scott in the streets and taverns, and William Blake shocked the gentry by painting naked in his garden on Sunday and Bill Shakespeare had his days truly in the round; and at night and on certain holy days we would tell stories of nightmare spirits, pieces of the dead come home and gone again come morning light. But these are not just those stories, not hardly; for they have passed through the lens of Mr. Bolivar's mind, and that passage changed them. They are made new, they are different, they are weird.

There is so much within this book, it beggars the mind. Core to many of the stories is the archetypal figure of Weird Jack, Jack the Balladeer, Jack the Giant Killer, and Jack Drake. Jack be nimble Jack be quick, Jack best be packing a heavy stick, for there are more than Cornish giants here to fight and fright, there are witches and black magic, deviltry and devils and even the Devil himself, Old Scratch whose hand should seldom be taken and damn well never shook.

Jack in one of his incarnations as Jack Drake commands our attention. In "The Lay of Jackson Drake," we witness Childe Jackson (you hear the old sounds? the child of Jack, Jack's son?) come to his father's manse deep in a haunted wood with a silver key, a key that fit not just the door of the house he sought but the very gate of Time itself, through multiple gates of Hell up through its very mouth, with more adventures in between than Khayyam could cram into twenty Rubaiyats. And that's just one of the ballads in the book! Here, just listen:

> And down the road a carny came;
> A barker ran his mouth.
> "Folks, come and see the spectacle!
> The Wonder of the South.
>
> "See He/She/It arrayed in chains,
> A horned three-headed freak,
> A giant from a fairy tale—
> You'll want to take a peek.

"Here liontamers, girls with beards,
  And oddities abound.
All tickets are a dollar, folks,
  The cheapest show around."

Then by a shoestring puppet show,
  Childe Jackson met a girl.

I'll leave it there, since we all know where that one goes.

Proceeding with the incredible literary journey that is this book, hundreds of pages later we encounter another of Bolivar's masterpieces, "The Rime of the Eldritch Mariner." It is of course a clever spin on Coleridge's *Rime of the Ancient Mariner*, fused with Bolivar's Lovecraftian sensibilities, and it is delicious stuff. The first stanza is pure ecstasy to any devotee of Lovecraft, and as one wades delightedly through each succeeding quatrain there are more Lovecraftian Easter eggs than one might find in a nameless Providence black magic barrio bodega at midnight. Yes, Providence has a barrio; it is Atwell's Avenue where the Al Son de Mi Barrio Food Truck can be found.

Lastly I must mention Bolivar's uncanny ability to bridge poetic and prosodic narrative into one hermetic whole. I called it melding, but it is really more than that; it is transmutation by literary alchemy whereby something is made that is greater than either of its parents. His ballads are superb, his stories scarcely less so, but by using both forms to tell a single narrative he achieves what the Surrealists wished for when they sought the perfect unity between what we call reality and what we call dream as a sort of super-reality. Hence the term Surrealism or super-realism, and it is just that same metaphysical ambivalence of hands under hot water/hands under cold water/hands under hot water again that Bolivar uses to cast us adrift into strange waters delightfully without a rowboat. But fear not, we are in safe hands, although at times we may feel as though we are drowning in delicious Weird.

I have deliberately not given you many of Bolivar's words. They are magic jewels and should be retrieved only by personal search; but you won't regret the journey. There are many doors to open and many keys to use, silver keys and emerald keys, and just when you imagine you have found and used the last, another glistens 'mid the gloamy gardinels and you must enter, you are lost.

Buy this book, read it and keep it and cherish it, lend it only to lovers, and if someone tries to steal it you should kick them out of your house.

Musings Philosophical and Religious

Donald Sidney-Fryer

ALAN GULLETTE. *Reviving a Dead Priest*. Oakland, CA: translucent books, 2018. 120 pp. $9.95 tpb.

As an elder in the community of poets who have contributed to the "Hippocampus Press Library of Poetry" (thus under the name of the seahorse as tutelary beast), it has been our great pleasure to watch new figures in the poetic genre of fantasy and science fiction, or science fantasy, emerge, grow, develop. Some we know as personal friends, and others at least as cordial acquaintances, encountered at conventions and similar events; some over the long term, and others only briefly (but significantly) so far.

Thus we have long known, or known of, Richard Tierney, Ann K. Schwader, and Alan Gullette; now more recently Ashley Dioses, K. A. Opperman, and Wade German; a few poets only through correspondence. Alan Gullette in addition has functioned as our long-term collaborator, without whose irreplaceable help some dozen books of ours could never have seen print—his indispensable help as a computer specialist.

Besides having books published by other houses, Gullette has appeared as part of those writers made public by Hippocampus Press under the enlightened aegis of owner-editor Derrick Hussey centered in New York City: in Gullette's case with *Intimations of Unreality*. This poet and author has built up an impressive corpus of literary works over the years. We here append the chief titles. *Another Eucharist* (1995); *From a Safe Distance* (2000); *Intimations of Unreality* (2012); *The Lighthouse Above the Graveyard* (with John Allen, 2016); *The Adventures of Franco Corelli* (2017); *I Grew These Hueless Clouds in the Dreary South* (2017); *Short Shrift* (2017); *Pantaleon* (2018). Most of these are poetry, with some as a mixture of poetry and prose. While they are basically free verse in free form, Gullette yet presents his poems in highly disciplined lines formed into regular verse paragraphs. The overall effect: liberated traditional, but still modern, very much so.

We have here now for inspection and experiencing at length a copy of his latest book of poetry, *Reviving a Dead Priest*. To give it overall shape, Gullette has organized the volume with the story-line of a religious teacher or priest. This guru dies and leaves as a legacy only his poems. His followers are perplexed as to what to do, but they have evidently given the poems to Alan as a sympathetic amanuensis and/or editor, who has now presented them as the book in hand. This all shapes up into a plausible scenario for the volume's raison d'être. Establishing the tone of the poetry in the collection, on the back of this trade handsome trade paperback (which features the striking portrait, a piece of art, showing some Far Eastern monk or priest), Alan quotes from the Japanese Buddhist priest Dogen Zenji: "He has plucked out the eye of the buddha ancestors and sat down inside that eye."

It is a generous collection, containing over seventy poems, including three pages of aphorisms as the antepenultimate selection that includes quite a few fascinating insights and pensées. The author, also the editor, has arranged the mostly short poems into the following sections: "Death and Life," "Initiation," "Of Seeming and Being," "Light from the East," "Reflections on Time," "Tabernacle Fire," "Five Prayers and a Psalm," "Revival," "The End." Short poems and short lines abound, often aphoristic in thought and feeling. Because, as the titles above indicate, the poet deals with subjects of the greatest weight and often fear, the presentation favored by the author comes across as light-hearted and thus reduces the dread and fear often aroused by such topics.

In this way the poetry becomes accessible and easy of approach, and the author maintains an amazing directness and clarity. By such a method he avoids needless confusion and complexity, a remarkable accomplishment in view of the heaviness of the subject matter. Thus he shows that if he has indeed imbibed some of the wisdom of the Far East, especially that of India. This wisdom probably shows up best in the longer poems: "The Blood Sutra," "Pontus and the Nagas," "Samantabhadra Takes a Nap," and "Tabernacle Fire." These four narratives are all wisdom fables, demonstrating much play, whimsy, irony, and humor. In fact, this characteristic sense of humor, not blatant but comfortable and relaxed, animates much of the volume, as do the title and the book's overall concept. Who would wish to revive a dead priest?—except metaphorically.

As the final stanza of "The Dead Priest" expresses it succinctly: "If the priest's unspoken words / Escape the funeral pyre, / Who will hear them?" (The poem's own quotation marks.) But let us quote a little bit from here and there throughout the volume to give the reader a feeling for the poet's unique sense of existential fun! (These quotes are mostly the conclusions of the pieces from which we cite.)

From "The Face of Doom":

> There are two things
>   that I can say of him:
> He is fixed in purpose,
>   and his grip is firm . . .

From "Funeral Rites":

> A great day to be alive!
> A great day to die!
> A great day to be buried!
> A great day to be revived!

From "Seer":

> Who has borne the burden of beauty
> Back from the realms sublime?

An entire brief poem, *"Poiema"* [Greek, a thing made]:

> Time lends Life's Spinner
> and descends

Three eyes see I
what is
What could be

One cries with sorrow
One laughs with joy
One sees

From "Incantation:":

Life exists not in time
But in the moment
The moment exists not in time
But in space

From "The Universe Breathes":

Take a breath—
The universe is breathing!
Take a breath
And hold it still . . .

From "The Fundament":

In everything, there is nothing;
In nothing, there is everything.
That's the fundamental truth.

In closing the section of direct quotations, we can do no better than to cite in full the two last poems in the collection. The first is "Giving Thanks":

I would like to thank
My mother and father
—and all the mothers and fathers before them—
For bringing me *here*.

I would also like to thank
Mother Earth and Father Sky,

Brother Sun and Sister Moon,
The Milky Way and all the Stars—
And the Big Bang.

And last, but not least,
I would like to thank
The Big Silence
That surrounds it all.

The second is "The Master Appeared":

The master appeared to me in a dream.

"There is precious little that you can do
To revive a dead priest. But the living—
They may have a chance."

Thus in many of these truly metaphysical poems the poet expresses diverse musings and fancies that many of us have entertained at times, but he has rendered us, poets and non-poets alike, a real service in doing so in such a lucid and accessible manner. We personally find this volume a godsend or a cosmos-gift of clarity in terms of the ongoing existential maelstrom and confusion. And for that we thank the author for *Reviving a Dead Priest*. Religion is not dead either officially or unofficially! But religious thought, to be genuine, must include a healthy skepticism.

All that we can do here, as well as with previous books, is to urge the enlightened reader to seek further enlightenment as purveyed in this enlightening volume. How the master or the messenger on the book's ˙ front cover appears beautifully dark-skinned, he who brings the message of enlightenment with its promise of spiritual light! This book exercised a positively therapeutic effect on us: and as experienced in strict sequence over the course of a single day of concentrated reading, it changed our consciousness. We cannot ask for anything more than that from any book, and especially from a book of poetry. The sense of fantasy and linguistic play holds high carnival in this volume!

Notes on Contributors

Manuel Arenas is what Howard Phillips Lovecraft would have called an "epicure of the terrible." He currently resides on Phoenix, Arizona, where he pens his Gothic fantasies and dark ditties sheltered behind heavy curtains, as he shuns the oppressive orb which glares down on him from the cloudless, dust-filled desert sky.

Chelsea Arrington has a predilection for things dark and romantic. Among her favorite authors are Algernon Charles Swinburne, Lord Dunsany, and Ray Bradbury. She likes her steaks rare and her wine as dry as graveyard dirt. Her poetry has appeared in the anthology *Folk Horror Revival: Corpse Roads*, *Spectral Realms* No. 8, and *The Audient Void* No. 5. She lives in Southern California with her boyfriend, her nephew, and two lap dogs.

David Barker has published two collections of Lovecraftian fiction written in collaboration with W. H. Pugmire: *The Revenant of Rebecca Pascal* and *In the Gulfs of Dream and Other Lovecraftian Tales*. They have also collaborated on the forthcoming Lovecraftian novel, *Witches in Dreamland*. Recently, David's work has appeared in *Cyäegha*, *Weird Fiction Review*, *The Audient Void*, *Nightmare's Realm*, and *Forbidden Knowledge*.

Leigh Blackmore has written weird verse since age thirteen. He has lived in the Illawarra, New South Wales, Australia, for the last decade. He has edited *Terror Australis: Best Australian Horror* (1993) and *Midnight Echo 5* (2011) and written *Spores from Sharnoth & Other Madnesses* (2008). A nominee for SFPA's Rhysling Award (Best Long Poem), Leigh is also a four-time Ditmar Award nominee. He is currently assembling an edition of *The Selected Letters of Robert Bloch*.

Benjamin Blake was born in the July of 1985, and grew up in the small town of Eltham, New Zealand. He is the author of the novel *The Devil's Children* and the poetry and prose collections *Southpaw Nights* and *Standing on the Threshold of Madness*.

Adam Bolivar, a native of Boston now residing in Portland, Oregon, published his weird fiction and poetry in the pages of *Nameless*, the *Lovecraft eZine*, *Spectral Realms*, and Chaosium's *Steampunk Cthulhu* and *Atomic Age Cthulhu* anthologies. His latest collection, *The Lay of Old Hex*, was published in 2017 by Hippocampus Press.

Fred Chappell is a distinguished American novelist and poet who has written extensively in the vein of weird and Lovecraftian fiction. His novel *Dagon* (Harcourt, 1968) was named the best foreign-language book by the Académie Française, and his story collection *More Shapes Than One* (St. Martin's Press, 1991) is entirely devoted to the weird. Several weird poems are included in an omnibus of his work from Centipede Press (2014).

Frank Coffman is professor of English, journalism, and creative writing at Rock Valley College in Rockford, Illinois. His primary interests as a critic are in the rise and relevance of popular imaginative literature across the genres of adventures, detection and mystery, fantasy, horror and the supernatural, and science fiction. He has published several articles on these genres and is the editor of Robert E. Howard's *Selected Poems*.

Scott J. Couturier hails from the far frigid lands of Northern Michigan. A novelist, poet, rock-'n'-roll archivist, and editor, his work has recently appeared in such venues as *The Audient Void, Feverish Fiction,* and the weird fiction anthology *Test Patterns*. In 2017 he released *The Curse of Roc-Thalian,* the third volume in his ongoing dark fantasy series *The Magistricide.*

Deborah L. Davitt was raised in Reno, Nevada, but received her M.A. in English from Penn State. She currently lives in Houston with her husband and son. She is known for her Edda-Earth novels, Pushcart- and Rhysling-nominated poetry, and short story publications.

Ashley Dioses is a writer of dark fiction and poetry from southern California. Her fiction and poetry has appeared in *Weird Fiction Review, Spectral Realms, Xnoybis, Weirdbook, Gothic Blue Book,* and elsewhere. Her debut collection of dark traditional poetry, *Diary of a Sorceress,* was published in 2017 by Hippocampus Press.

J. T. Edwards was born and raised, where he still resides, in East Tennessee. He found solace in the weird and macabre at a young age, watching shows such as *The Twilight Zone*. His later discovery of the works of H. P. Lovecraft, Clark Ashton Smith, Thomas Ligotti, and Austrian expressionist poet Georg Trakl, to name a few, proved monumental in keeping him going through dark times and furthering his imagination.

Poems by **Kendall Evans** have appeared in *Weird Tales, Analog, Asimov's,* and other magazines. His stories have appeared in *Amazing, Weirdbook, Fantastic,* and elsewhere. His novel *The Rings of Ganymede,* a ring cycle in the tradition of Wagner's operas and Tolkien's *Lord of the Rings,* is now available (Alban Lake Books, 2014).

Michael Fantina had numerous poems published in North America, the United Kingdom, and Australia. Three of his chapbooks are currently available from Rainfall Books in the UK, and a major selection, *Alchemy of Dreams,* was published by Hippocampus Press in 2017.

Ian Futter began writing stories and poems in his childhood, but only lately has started to share them. One of his poems appears in Jason V Brock's anthology *The Darke Phantastique* (Cycatrix Press, 2014), and he continues to produce dark fiction for admirers of the surreal.

Liam Garriock is an author and poet who counts authors such as Kafka, Arthur Machen, J. G. Ballard, Lovecraft, William S. Burroughs, Borges, Poe, William Blake, and Philip K. Dick as among his many touchstones. He lives in Edinburgh, Scotland.

Wade German is the author of *Dreams from a Black Nebula* (Hippocampus Press, 2014). His poetry has been nominated for the Pushcart, Rhysling, and Elgin awards, and has received numerous honorable mentions in Ellen Datlow's *Best Horror of the Year* anthologies.

Originally from Connecticut, **David B. Harrington** is a proud resident of Portland, Oregon. He enjoys reading and writing as well as playing tennis and the bass guitar. David's work has been published in various magazines and anthologies, including *New Myths, Lovecraftiana, Hypertomb, Sirens Call eZine,* and *Eldritch Tales* (Necronomicon Press).

Michelle Jeffrey has been writing poetry, prose, and short stories from a very young age. She is a regular contributor to pagan magazines in Australia. Her mother introduced her to horror movies and read horror stories to her as a young girl, sparking off a lifelong love of the horror genre.

Marcos Legaria is a scholar on H. P. Lovecraft, R. H. Barlow, Clark Ashton Smith, and related writers. His articles have appeared in the *Lovecraft Annual* and elsewhere.

Charles Lovecraft is a resident of Sydney, where he studies English at Macquarie University. He started writing in 1972, inspired by George Orwell. He began writing in earnest in 1975, inspired momentously by H. P. Lovecraft. As publisher-editor, Charles began P'rea Press in 2007 to publish weird and fantastic poetry, criticism, and bibliography, and to keep traditional poetry forms alive (www.preapress.com). He has edited thirty-one books.

Michael D. Miller is an adjunct professor and NEH medievalist summer scholar with numerous one-act play productions and awards, including several optioned screenplays to his credit. He has written the Realms of Fantasy RPG for Mythopoeia Games Publications. He has also been a writer of poems for many years, yet only recently started circulating them. This issue of *Spectral Realms* marks his weird verse debut in print.

Charles D. O'Connor III is a weird poet living in Virginia Beach, Va. He has an extensive collection of rare fiction material and runs a Facebook page dedicated to R. H. Barlow. "Life can be difficult," he says, "but weird fiction saved my life, and has been good to me. I'll always be good to it."

K. A. Opperman is a poet with a predilection for the strange, the Gothic, and the grotesque, continuing the macabre and fantastical tradition of such luminaries as Poe, Clark Ashton Smith, and H. P. Lovecraft. His first verse collection, *The Crimson Tome*, was published by Hippocampus Press in 2015.

Russ Parkhurst was born to human parents on November 30, 1953. A strange and quiet child, he was a dreamer and an artist where most of his peers were farmers and common laborers. In his later years he achieved multiple college degrees and became a lifelong practitioner of the martial arts. Shunned by his neighbors as a weirdo, he lives not by himself in an old house filled with ghosts in the American Midwest.

Manuel Pérez-Campos's poetry has appeared previously in *Spectral Realms* and *Weird Fiction Review*. A collection of his poetry in the key of the weird is in progress; so is a collection of ground-breaking essays on H. P. Lovecraft. He lives in Bayamón, Puerto Rico.

Allan Rozinski is a writer of speculative poetry and fiction whose poems have been recently published in the *Horror Writers Association Poetry Showcase, Volume IV: Bête Noire* and the *Literary Hatchet*. His poem "In the Labyrinth"—published in *Eternal Haunted Summer* (Winter Solstice 2017)—was nominated for the 2018 Rhysling Award in the long form and is included in *The 2018 Rhysling Anthology.*

Jessica Amanda Salmonson is the author of the heroic fantasy trilogy *The Tomoe Gozen Saga* and the nonfiction work *The Encyclopedia of Amazons.* Her short story collections include *A Silver Thread of Madness* and *The Deep Museum: Ghost Stories of a Melancholic.* Her poetry has appeared in a Rhysing Awards anthology and in Ellen Datlow and Terri Windling's *The Year's Best Fantasy and Horror.*

Ann K. Schwader lives and writes in Colorado. Her most recent collections are *Dark Energies* (P'rea Press, 2015) and *Twisted in Dream* (Hippocampus Press, 2011). Her *Wild Hunt of the Stars* (Sam's Dot, 2010) and *Dark Energies* were Bram Stoker Award finalists. She is also a two-time Rhysling Award winner (2010 and 2015) and was the Poet Laureate for NecronomiCon Providence 2015.

Darrell Schweitzer is a short story writer and novelist, and former coeditor of *Weird Tales.* He has published much humorous Lovecraftian verse (*Non Compost Mentis* [Zadok Allen, 1993] et al.) and also has two serious poetry collections in print, *Groping toward the Light* (Wildside Press, 2000) and *Ghosts of Past and Future* (Wildside Press, 2008).

John Shirley is the author of *Lovecraft Alive!*, a collection of Lovecraftian stories from Hippocampus Press, the Bram Stoker Award–winning story collection *Black Butterflies: A Flock on the Dark Side*, and the classic horror novels *Demons* and *Cellars*.

Donald Sidney-Fryer is the author of *Songs and Sonnets Atlantean* (Arkham House, 1971), *Emperor of Dreams: A Clark Ashton Smith Bibliography* (Donald M. Grant, 1978), *The Atlantis Fragments* (Hippocampus Press, 2009), and many other volumes. He has edited Smith's *Poems in Prose* (Arkham House, 1965) and written many books and articles on California poets. His autobiography *Hobgoblin Apollo* (2016) and two volumes of miscellany, *Aesthetics Ho!* (2017) and *West of Wherevermore* (2018) have been published by Hippocampus Press.

Christina Sng is an award-winning poet, writer, and artist. Her work has been published in numerous print and online venues worldwide and garnered more than 70 awards and nominations, including the 2018 Jane Reichhold International Prize. She is the author of *A Constellation of Songs*, *Catku*, Elgin Chapbook Award nominees *An Assortment of Sky Things*, *Astropoetry*, and Bram Stoker Award winner *A Collection of Nightmares*.

Tatiana is a Gothic musician from Berlin. Aside from playing and composing music she also occasionally plays small roles in theatrical works of the underground scene in Berlin. She is a strong supporter of animal rights and often takes part in demonstrations against animal abuse and all other injustice.

M. F. Webb's poetry has appeared in previous issues of *Spectral Realms*, and her fiction has been published in *Latchkey Tales*. She hails from a Victorian seaport town in Washington State, which luckily is not too much like Innsmouth.

Mary Krawczak Wilson has written poetry, fiction, plays, articles, and essays. She was born in St. Paul, Minnesota, and moved to Seattle in 1991. Her most recent essay appeared in the *American Rationalist*.

CPSIA information can be obtained
at www.ICGtesting.com
Printed in the USA
LVHW010357060319
609669LV00019B/1082

9 781614 982289